NORDIC NOIR

14 Unsolved True Crime Cases

MICHAEL EAST

DEDICATION

For my late grandmother Jennifer who would have been very proud. For my mother Sarah, who's love of true crime set in on this path, and for Hope, who has entertained many a crazy theory.

"Make the best of what you've got, don't complicate
things unnecessarily, and hate coincidence."

- Leif G.W. Persson

CONTENTS

Lilly Lindeström. Public domain.

1 THE VAMPIRE KILLING OF LILLY LINDESTRÖM

Sweden, 1932

When the word "vampire" is mentioned, people have a very vivid image in their minds. To some, it's the hideously twisted form of Nosferatu. To others, the murderous charm of Christopher Lee. To younger readers, perhaps it may be the young romantic Edward Cullen of the *Twilight* franchise. However, vampirism is not something limited to fiction. The legends surrounding Countess Elizabeth Báthory and modern-day vampire cults show that blood-drinking has a real and very long human history.

As of 2010, over 50,000 people have appeared in psychiatric literature who were obsessed with drinking blood. The condition is popularly known as Renfield's syndrome. Clinical vampirism is rarely described and usually forms part of a more conventional psychiatric diagnosis such as schizophrenia or paraphilia. While most those with the condition can seemingly control their desires or have sought adequate treatment, several serial killers have utilized blood drinking in their modus operandi, including the notorious Peter Kürten and Richard Chase.

Into these legends and the truth behind them comes Lilly Lindeström. Some believe that the case shows real vampires are still at work in Europe; others say it is a deranged killer, another potential Peter Kürten style murderer. However, the truth might just be that the killing was neither of these things and that the killing of Lilly Lindeström has become more myth than reality.

On May 4, 1932, Minnie Jansson became concerned for the wellbeing of her friend, Lilly Lindeström. Both women were prostitutes in the Atlas area of Stockholm, and Minnie hadn't seen or heard from Lilly for three days, despite attempts to telephone her and frantic knocks on her door. Lilly was known as "the Call Girl," a pun on her lifestyle and the fact she was the only telephone owner in the building.

She had been born in Malmö on August 29, 1900, marrying young and divorcing almost as quickly, moving to Stockholm at the age of 22. While the 1920s were a time of optimism and opportunity, the Great Depression of the 1930s turned many lives on their head, not least that of Lilly Lindeström. Forced into prostitution through the harshness of the times, Lilly had been escorting since April of 1931. She did well for herself, avoiding the streets, and instead utilized her telephone to make bookings out of the perceived safety of her flat. She was known to the police yet remained a popular figure with those who knew her. She had enough money to buy luxury items such as a radio and even purchased clothes on credit at local stores.

Lilly's life seemed stable and even prosperous, considering the times she lived in. Her circumstance allowed a certain amount of leisure time, and both Lilly and Minnie had discussed their evening plans to attend celebrations at Djurgården. This island forms part of the Royal National Park. Their conversation was interrupted when Lindeström received a strange call on this same phone, asking for a liaison. Minnie would later describe the voice as sounding "well-behaved" and like "a nice and sober gentleman." It was April 30, known in Sweden as Walpurgis Night.

"Can you receive me if I come in a while?" Asked the voice on the telephone, with Lilly responding to say, "Yes, are you far away?"
"No," said the man, as recanted by Minnie Jansson, "I'm very close. I'm coming soon."

An abbreviation of Saint Walpurgis Night, Walpurgis Night is the eve of the Christian feast day of Saint Walpurga. It is celebrated on the night of April 30 and into May 1. Walpurga was heralded by German Christians for his battles against pests and disease, also being hailed for his fight against witchcraft. Christians would thus pray for his intervention against witches and warlocks, and people still light bonfires to ward off evil on Saint Walpurga's Eve. In Sweden, the festival is a public event and marks the arrival of spring. Communal events include the lighting of bonfires, choral singing, and speeches by local celebrities to welcome the coming of the new season.

Writing in *The Golden Bough: A Study in Comparative Religion*, the Scottish anthropologist Sir James George Frazer said, "May 1 is a great popular festival in the more midland and southern parts of Sweden. On the eve of the festival, huge bonfires, which should be lighted by striking two flints together, blaze on all the hills and knolls."

Minnie had left the building to fetch some milk and, after returning around 7pm, found Lilly was entertaining the client in her cramped apartment. She came down to Minnie twice to enquire about condoms and confirmed it was the same man as the one on the telephone. She was nude except for a coat. It was the last Minnie had heard from her friend. At precisely 9pm, Minnie knocked on her door, asking if she wished to visit the bonfire at Djurgården as planned. There was no answer. Minnie assumed she had left with her client and headed out but couldn't spot her friend anywhere at the bonfire. Returning home, Minnie tried her door again. Still no answer.

After a male friend also failed to get in touch, the duo went to Ruth Jonsson, who, alongside her husband, were the landlords of the building. Together, they went to visit Emma Lundgren, another friend of Lilly's. Emma, likewise, hadn't seen Lilly since Walpurgis Night and noted that she had failed to meet with her as planned on May 2. Given the ever-present threats from dangerous clients, they decided to contact the police on the 4th. Officer Nordström of the Stockholm Police was first on the scene and, failing to also get an answer at the door, called the fire department to force an entry. What they found when they broke into the apartment would shock Sweden — Lilly Lindeström had been murdered.

Lilly's apartment as viewed from the outside and featured in the June 28, 1950 edition of *Aftonbladet*.

Lying face down on an ottoman, her clothes were folded neatly on a chair next to her naked corpse, and three sofa cushions were stacked on top of the body. The apartment was tidy and cleaned. She had suffered severe trauma to the head from three massive blows and had already been dead for two to three days when the body was discovered.

Working at the scene, the police district doctor, Dr. Ternell, believed the murder weapon was a crowbar, pipe, or another similar heavy metal object, and Lilly had been attacked from behind, likely killing her instantly. She may have been assaulted while engaged in a sex act. A blood-soaked tea towel was found in the kitchen, and friends noted that nothing was missing from the apartment. The killer brought the weapon with him and took it as he left, showing evident premeditation.

Led by police chief Alvar Zetterquist, detectives likely initially believed it was a clear case of another prostitute murdered by her client. However, they were intrigued by the amount of saliva on Lilly's neck and body, not to mention the fact that she had allegedly somehow been exsanguinated — drained of blood. There was only a tiny amount of blood at the scene, with none on the walls, furnishings, or floor and no noticeable puncture pounds to the body. Despite legends, a gravy ladle "used to drink her blood" was not found at the scene, with the object entering the narrative much later.

The Atlas neighborhood was heavily industrialized, with the entire area being named after the industrial company Atlas AB whose workshops littered the area.

The flats here were small and dark, adjoining Saint Erik's Plaza. The Plaza today has undergone significant gentrification, with apartment prices being among the most expensive in Stockholm. Yet, in the early 20th century, Saint Erik's Plaza was considered a "prostitute's stroll" where liaisons would be arranged with punters.

Adding immediate weight to the theory that Lilly had fallen prey to one of her clients was the fact that a condom was found protruding from the victim's anus, with three other wrappers found in the bin. The killer had taken the rest of the pack that Minnie had given her friend.

There were no witnesses to anyone being seen at the apartment after the believed time of death, and nobody heard a struggle. Lindeström's landlady saw five men coming and going before this, and the fact that Lilly returned to her friend for a second condom leads to speculation that the killer was, in fact, not the "gentleman" that Minnie had heard on the phone. However, a suspect who may have been the killer was spotted at Norma's Cafe in Sankt Eriksplan with a waitress noticing that a man who came in at 9pm brought a porcelain container with him that she knew belonged to Lilly. The man ordered two steak dinners and left.

Interestingly, the morning after the murder, the apartment next door was burgled. A woman was woken at 5am by a young man attempting to access a locked storage closet. The woman screamed, with the man quickly trying to muffle her. Escaping, she ran down the stairs and cried out for the police. However, when the nearby patrol officer had reached the apartment, the would-be burglar was gone. He was described as wearing a suit, but no hat and coat, leading to some speculation he was somebody from within the building. Police dismissed the incident as a coincidence, noting that no robbery was suspected in the case of Lilly Lindeström.

Six weeks after the killing, a stained ladle was found outside the apartment building, with many believing the stains were blood. It was too light to be the murder weapon. Still, a subsequent story in the newspaper *Aftonbladet* claimed that it had been utilized to drink the blood of Lindeström. They claimed that the tiny amount of blood at the scene, with none on the walls, furnishings, or floor, had led police to believe that the killer had drunk there using the ladle, brazenly carrying the rest of her blood away. The local press was in uproar, with sensationalist headlines dubbing the killer "the Atlas Vampire" as pressure mounted on the police to catch a suspect. It is worth noting that the ground floor of Lilly Lindeström's apartment was a restaurant where a ladle would not be unusual.

These sensationalist headlines came in the wake of the Peter Kürten killings in Germany and at the height of the Universal horror craze. Kürten's crimes had shocked Europe. His 1929 series of macabre sex assaults and killings had won him the nickname of "The Vampire of Düsseldorf" as he had attempted to drink the blood of his victims. He was executed in July of 1931, just five months after the release of Universal's *Dracula* starring Bela Lugosi. The film is a classic of horror on film, being a cornerstone of cinematic vampire movies. It was both a commercial and critical success, and on May 6, 1932, the German movie *Vampyr* had its premiere. The public was eager to read anything linked to these legends or the monstrous crimes of Kürten. Monsters sold well at the news-stands. The claims of vampirism would be resurrected in 1950 when *Aftonbladet* interviewed retired investigator John Berg, Berg claiming that the ladle had been found wrapped in a bloody tea-towel at the scene. The sensation started all over again.

Desperate, the police arrested a pimp, Pettersson, after his own wife raised suspicions. Having allegedly been seen covered in blood by his spouse, the police held the man for 10 days. They released him after his alibi checked out with his business partner, yet this was always said to be shaky at best. Meanwhile, a man with whom Lindeström had had an affair, Ragnar Nilsson, was likewise eliminated. There were virtually no clues to go on. Nothing had been stolen from the apartment, and the killer had left nothing behind. While there were fingerprints, there were many sets, and they were impossible to identify. Lilly's address book turned up nothing and what other evidence existed was useless, with DNA evidence on the saliva and condom decades away from being possibly utilized as a clue.

Police were hopeful that the killer may have an attack of conscience and come forward but also feared that this was unlikely to have been the murderer's first killing nor his last. Concerned they were dealing with a serial killer, they waited for him to strike again, fearing for an innocent life somewhere in Stockholm but hopeful that he may yield more clues next time.

The days turned into weeks and soon months and years. The "Atlas Vampire" seemingly never struck again.

In the decades since the brutal killing, many theories have emerged surrounding what may have happened in that tiny Stockholm room. Many believe that, if the claims of exsanguination are correct, few men would have had the knowledge to make such an effective and clean evacuation of blood. Given that "almost all" of Lilly Lindeström's blood had apparently been expelled, the killer would have needed to be both bold in carrying it through the streets and equally need a place to store it. Equally, the risk of clotting would require speed, suggesting perhaps a culprit within the same building. However, with no puncture wounds on the body, there is significant doubt about the claim's veracity. Speaking on the Swedish TV show *Crime of the Week* in 2012, criminologist and author Leif GW Persson stated that he doesn't believe that the body was, in fact, exsanguinated. He also noted that the stains on the ladle were never positively identified as blood. Persson believes that Lilly knew her killer.

Another popular theory was that the murderer may have been a police officer or somehow otherwise involved in police work, with the murder weapon being a police baton. The scene was effectively scrubbed of clues long before the police became busy.

With little evidence ever being found in the case and the "Atlas Vampire" having seemingly never struck again, there is little hope of ever finding out the truth behind the killing of Lilly Lindeström. While there may be some truth somewhere in the body being drained of blood, the retellings of the Lindeström murder have often lost sight of the story at the core. They focus on the myths of vampirism rather than on the tragedy of Lilly Lindeström herself. It is not a charming and suave Christopher Lee story, one charged with eroticism and passion. Nor is it a myth. It is the story of a woman, fallen on hard times, who was bludgeoned to death while entertaining a client, likely for a sexual thrill. While not the answer many seek, the sad truth is, sensationalism sells just as well today as it did in 1932.

Lilly's Lindeström's body was returned to Malmö and buried in the Eastern Cemetery of the city. She never received justice and deserved more than being a damsel in yet another 1930s vampire story.

2 THE STRANGE DISAPPEARANCE OF VIOLA WIDEGREN

Sweden, 1948

Young people running away from violent broken families is unfortunately not an unusual story. Many women and children run away to new lives as they are torn between violence and a leap into the unknown. Some make it, yet others suffer further violence when they are returned home, often by friends, family, or the police. Vulnerable and frequently desperate, many more fall into even worse situations such as new violent relationships, prostitution, or other forms of exploitation.

While by no means perfect, there are numerous support networks available for people to escape domestic violence in our own era. Yet, in 1948, such violence was seen almost as a right for men, used to subdue wives and children. So when a daughter became sick of her violent father and promised to run away, many believed she had done just that. Only, she never returned home, and decades on, the strange disappearance of Viola Widegren remains one of Sweden's most enduring mysteries.

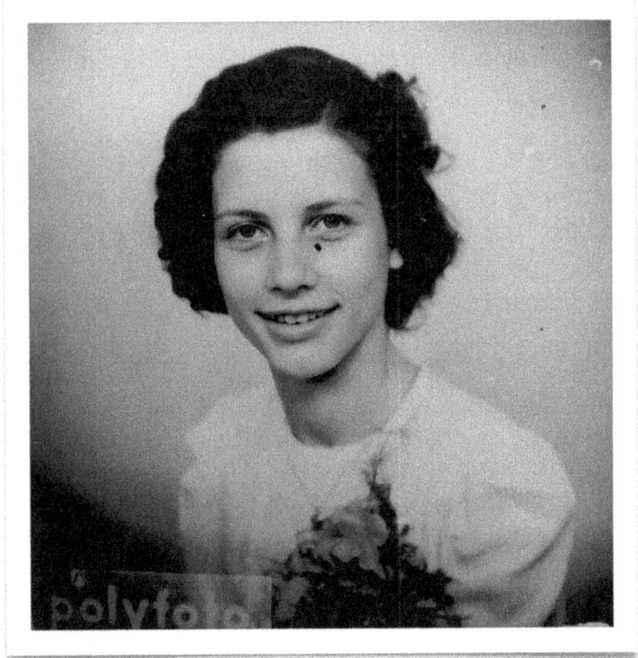

Viola Widegren. Public domain.

Viola "Vivi" Widegren was born on May 2, 1931. She was a health care assistant and grew up on a farm in Västerbränna, Sweden. Her parents had previously run a small business and moved into the area after her mother became seriously ill through diabetes and tuberculosis. Viola's father, Karl Widegren, worked as a timber surveyor and carer, looking after his daughter and sick wife, his single income no doubt making life difficult.

Viola's mother eventually died in 1937 when she was six, and her father subsequently remarried in 1938, having another daughter, a half-sister to Viola. Despite limitations, the family was able to buy a new property in 1944 and a few years afterward even added a second, renting it out to a mother and her two children.

Speaking with the Swedish newspaper *Expressen* in 2018, a former roommate said that Viola had described her father as strict and pious.

"She was pretty quiet by herself. She was dark and handsome, but there was never any talk of any guys," the roommate recalled. "We went to the movies sometimes or just checked the shop windows in town. But I never saw her look at a boy."

Viola had been studying for her high school diploma since 1946, and as a 17-year-old, she was expected to complete her studies in the spring of 1949. According to one friend, Viola had confided in her that her revision was not going well. In early 1948, she became interested in healthcare work after a stay in the hospital. By that October, Viola had gained a temporary position as a medical assistant at the Garrison Hospital in Sollefteå.

The job at Garrison Hospital was a live-in position, and Viola moved into the dormitories at the hospital, promising her parents that she would continue her school diploma and return home when she had the opportunity. Everyone there had their own bed, with a desk and dresser to share. The other rooms were likewise shared, including a kitchen, bathroom, and separate toilets.

On Friday, December 3, 1948, Viola received her salary, a modest income of 365 Swedish Krona, around £600/$800 in today's money. The job ended the day afterward, but she was given a week's extension starting on Monday, December 6. Calling home, her parents agreed to the new week but believed she was beginning again immediately.

On Sunday, Viola got into an argument on the phone over the issue, her father believing she had lied to him about the date and demanding that she return immediately. Viola had seemingly asked to go to a party, exposing that she wasn't starting work till Monday. Whether she had deliberately deceived her father or the whole affair was merely a misunderstanding is unknown.

Frightened by her father, Viola told co-workers at the hospital that "if I get beaten up when I get home, I will not come back." She added that if her father found out about her poor school performance, she would be physically disciplined and banned from returning to the hospital. These statements all point to a controlling and abusive relationship in the household. However, there are no reports of prior violence or controlling behavior beyond these incidents. It also seems likely that Karl was overprotective of his daughter, being widowed and raising her from a young age without her real mother.

Viola seemingly spent Monday buying Christmas presents for her family and enjoying her time in the city, perhaps embracing life a little before the punishment she understood was coming. In Sollefteå, she had more freedom than at home and a more active social life. Subsequently, Viola's trips home were becoming more and more infrequent as she began to drift apart from her family and upbringing.

Returning home that same day as instructed, Viola was the victim of a violent confrontation with her father and, as she predicted, was beaten. According to the family's account, Viola started the fight, bursting in without greeting and acting "hysterical," shouting and waking Karl from a nap. The father was enraged at the verbal attack in his home, stating that Viola had no right to say such things after being away for a month. He demanded that she quit the hospital and dedicate herself to her diploma, her stepmother backing her husband. A police report from the time says that Viola was dragged by her hair into an alcove and had her pants pulled down. The father would smack her buttocks as if she were a child and then slap her about the head, causing a nosebleed. After sitting a while to stop the blood flow, Viola reportedly exited the front door without her hat or purse.

"I saw that she was bleeding. And the next day, there was blood on the ottoman. Her little sister had also told the school the next day what had happened," Viola's stepmother later told *Expressen*. "The last thing I saw was that Vivi was lying on the couch bleeding. He scolded her as she lay there on the couch, threatened and held her. But suddenly Viola sat up, got up, and ran out of the house."

Later, Karl Widegren decided to go and search for his daughter, realizing that it was December and freezing cold. He searched the immediate area and found nothing. Over the coming days, friends were called to assist in the search, but with no luck finding the missing Viola either. Her parents left it until Wednesday, December 8, to contact police, believing Viola had likely gone back to the hospital, perhaps asking her friends not to reveal where she was.

However, this wasn't the case, and the police began a more extensive search. Fearing the worst, the police checked nearby bus stations and searched both rivers and lakes. They questioned her family. Officially, the police said they had no suspicions of foul play, yet people in the village began to gossip that Viola had been murdered in her home.

Viola was under an immense amount of stress and pressure. By her own admission, she was failing in her studies which her family expected her to pass. The position she enjoyed was coming to an end. After spending much of her salary on Christmas presents for her father, stepmother, and half-sister, she had been violently assaulted with nobody seemingly standing up for her. Police began to work publicly on the theory that the young woman had either committed suicide in her despair or, attempting to scare her family, had died of exposure or had an accident. While the weather was around two degrees, it had recently reached minus levels and would do again in the coming days. The area around Viola's home was close to the Faxälven river, noted for its strong and rapidly changing currents. However, the police searched both the river and local forests, finding no trace of the missing girl.

Police divers search the river. Public domain.

In the years since 1948, there were sightings of Viola Widegren in the cities of Stockholm and Malmö, as well as both Spain and Canada. These sightings were reported right up until the 1980s. The veracity of these reports is uncertain, but some believe that Viola decided to leave her abusive household and problems and never come back. One bus driver questioned in 1948 said that he'd seen her on his bus in the hours after she disappeared, but he would later recant his story. Trains had departed for Stockholm and Östersund during that evening from the nearby town of Helgum. There were even more places that could have been a destination if she had indeed taken a bus. This is, after all, what she told friends she would do if she was beaten again. There was even a rumor that Viola had gone to Finland with a doctor who had got her pregnant.

Over the years, letters have been sent claiming to be from Viola, and whether these are genuine, the work of a prankster or a killer attempting to cover their tracks is open to speculation.

However, if she was going to make a new start with her life, it seems unlikely she would have left without her possessions or money. Equally, she would likely have told friends of her plan. Speaking in 1998, police investigator Janne Sundin cast doubt on this theory, stating that it was not in her personality to take such a course of action, with Viola being inexperienced and somewhat timid. Sundin prefers the view that Viola committed suicide.

The other theory is, of course, that Viola was murdered.

While she may have met a stranger following her departure from the family home, perhaps seeking comfort or shelter, most theories down this avenue point toward Karl Widegren as a likely culprit. Some of the claims are gruesome and possibly show how disliked the father was amongst the local community.

One witness swore that she had seen mason jars containing body parts in the Widegren's basement. Another said that thick black smoke seen coming from the home was clear evidence that a body was being burned, and a neighbor even suggested that Viola had been cannibalized and fed to the pigs at the farm. Despite these lurid claims, police extensively questioned the family, including the eight-year-old half-sister, and nobody raised any suspicions. However, it was noted that the father was reluctant to be fully honest about the argument with his daughter, toning down the violence. His lack of complete honesty got around the village and was one of the factors that led people to take against him. During the original investigation, police privately thought Viola had been the victim of a crime rather than succumbing to an accident or committing suicide. Until the day he died, Viola's father believed that he had already been convicted of a crime in the eyes of his peers.

Viola was declared legally dead in 1970, and the case has fascinated generations of Swedes. Indeed, this morbid curiosity has often pushed the boundaries of taste, with Viola's house in Västerbränna becoming a dark tourist destination. The house, "Villa Viola," was a bed and breakfast where you could spend the night before the building was sold to a private resident, a former childhood friend.

It is 72 years since anyone saw Viola Widegren alive, and, despite the sightings, it seems unlikely that anyone would have been able to hide their identity for that long, particularly a young woman with no access to resources to aid her. Sadly, it seems likely that Viola died the very same night she vanished into the cold Swedish air.

The story of Viola Widegren is, sadly, almost too

familiar. A young teenager who wanted more from life than what her background allowed her, one beholden to a violent household and looking for an escape. That escape seemingly came not from a new life in the city but through death in either a tragic undiscovered accident or through more sinister events. Perhaps, one day, bones or other remains may be found from Viola, finally putting to rest one of Sweden's most notorious disappearances.

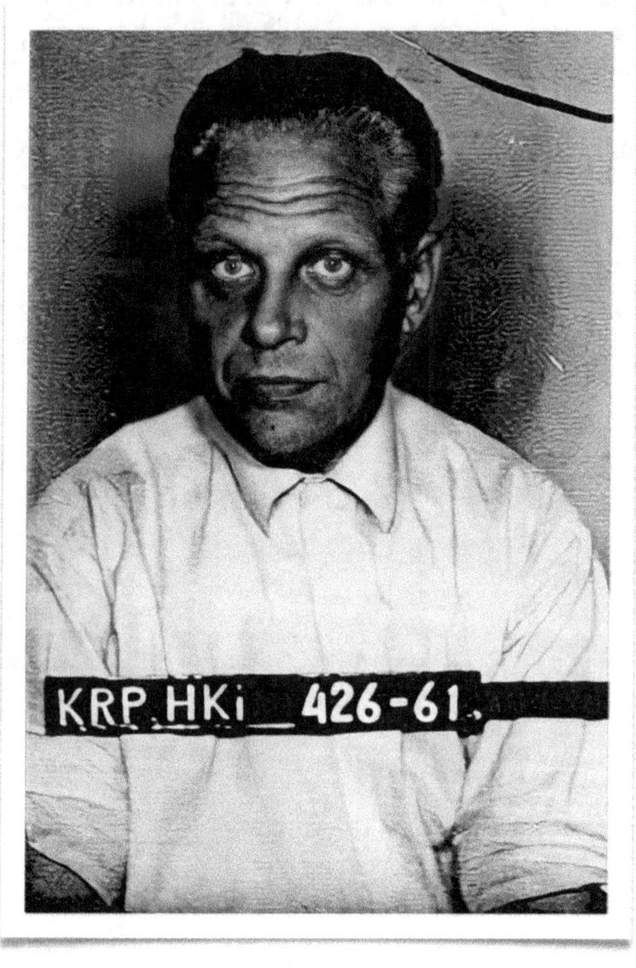

Hans Assmann mugshot, believed to be from 1960s. Public domain.

3 THE ALLEGED CRIMES OF HANS ASSMANN

Finland, 1953 - 1963

The following chapters deal with five of Finland's most infamous unsolved crimes, all connected through allegations leveled at a single individual: Hans Assmann.

Assmann is infused in the lore of Finnish true crime and, in many respects, exists as almost a boogeyman. He has been linked to numerous more killings than we shall cover here, where we will focus instead on the most famous. They are the 1953 murder of Kyllikki Saari, the 1955 slaying of Elli Immo, the double campsite murder at Tulilahti in 1959, the infamous Lake Bodom murders of 1960, and the 1963 killing of Sirkka-Liisa Valjus. Covering all five of those cases in the coming chapters, we shall first tell the Hans Assmann story to avoid repetition.

The first time Hans Assmann was ever on police radars for involvement in a serious crime was in 1960, following the Lake Bodom affair. Assmann had emigrated to Sweden and then Finland following the Second World War, and by 1960, he lived in the village of Bodom. On June 6, 1960, following the murders of two women and a man at the lake, Assmann turned up at Helsinki Surgical Hospital behaving unusually, said to be aggressive and nervous. He had red stains splattered on his clothes, and the doctor who treated him was confident that he had been the killer. Following a police sketch that bore an uncanny likeness, Assmann also cut his hair short.

Despite suspicion, Assmann maintained a solid alibi for the time of the killings, having been cheating on his wife at the time. He spent the night with his lover, and the two were not alone in the house, with multiple witnesses confirming he had been present and never left the residence. The witnesses said that he couldn't have left without being seen, and police never took his candidature as a suspect seriously. The truth is that the legend of Hans Assmann is mainly built on supposition and the public's willingness to believe a fantastical tale.

The theory that Assmann was involved was made popular with the public through a series of books published by the doctor who treated him, Professor Jorma Palo, the sensational work turning him into a one-man crime wave. Assmann, however, seemed to enjoy the infamy. By 1997, he was an alcoholic and nearing death, deciding to tell his life story to Matti

Paloaro, a former police officer and then editor of the Finnish true crime magazine *Alibi*.

Assmann revealed his story to Paloaro, recanting how he had been a member of the SS and served as a concentration camp guard at Auschwitz during the war. During his time at the camp, he fell in love with a Jewish girl and became disillusioned with life as a Nazi. When his liaison with the girl was discovered, he was sent to the eastern front to fight the advancing Soviets. There, he was captured and quickly turned, becoming a KGB agent.

He seemingly confessed to being involved in the 1953 murder of Kyllikki Saari, where a young woman was apparently kidnapped while bicycling home, her body being buried in a local swamp. Assmann indicated that it hadn't been a murder at all, and his chauffeur had accidentally hit the girl with their car. Claiming to have been a KGB agent, Assmann feared that their actual reason for being in the area would be revealed, and the duo staged the case as murder.

Assmann's ex-wife Vieno Assmann reported that he had been close to Isojoki at the time of Kyllikki's disappearance, and the suspect was known to own a cream Opel car like the one seen by a witness. She added that there were dents in this car after that night and that one of his socks was missing. A sock had been found close to the scene and was believed to have been used as a gag. Equally, on the night of Saari's disappearance, his shoes had been wet, and, by her account, a few days afterward, Assmann and his driver left with a shovel. Importantly, Assmann was left-handed, police having ascertained that the killer must have been so.

Assman himself, however, only ever gave hints and suggestions to Paloaro and how much of the tale is true is open to debate, with many suggesting that Assmann was nothing but a fantasist.

"One thing, however, I can tell you right away … because it is the oldest one, and in a way, it was an accident that had to be covered up. Otherwise, our trip would have been revealed," Assmann told Paloaro. "Even though my friend was a good driver, the accident was unavoidable. I assume you know what I mean."

Beyond the Kyllikki Saari killing, Assmann was named a suspect in the Tulilahti campsite murders by Paloaro on astonishingly thin evidence, primarily the fact that the case showed remarkable similarities to the Saari murder. The murders were brutal, with two young women, Riitta Pakkanen, 23, and Eine Nyyssönen, 21, being stabbed and bludgeoned to death inside their tent before being dragged away to be buried in a nearby swamp.

As with Kyllikki, Riitta had been killed with a heavy blow to the skull, which was covered up on burial. There may have been an element of stalking, but an opportunistic killer was likely. A grave had been dug in a bog with a shovel sourced close to the crime scene. Also just like with Kyllikki, the killer tried to disguise the site. The bicycles of the deceased had been hidden and submerged in both cases. It seems very possible that the killings were the work of the same individual or individuals.

Multiple witnesses close to Heinävesi said they saw two men together speaking German. They reportedly purchased a map for the Tulilahti campsite, and one of the two matched the description of Assmann. He always had a chauffeur, the man who, by his own admission, had run-down Kyllikki Saari. Upon investigations, Assmann's wife confirmed that her husband had been in Heinävesi during the murders and that he had visited the area several times previously, including the Tulilahti campsite.

The evidence to link Assmann to other crimes is even thinner and rests almost entirely on his own series of hints or his wife's allegations.

"I suppose you expect me to tell about those tent and knife things…." Assmann told Paloaro. "I have to disappoint you; I will not speak about the details; I will not admit nor deny things."

Was he referring to the Tulilahti murders or the Lake Bodom killings, for example?

The Lake Bodom killings saw two women and a man killed inside their tent in 1960, with another man surviving terrible injuries. Beyond the campsite element and use of both a knife and blunt instrument, very little connects the murders to the ones at the Tulilahti campsite. The Tulilahti killer entered the tent to carry out the crime, and the bodies were buried in that case, with an effort being made to cover up the murders. Here, the killer struck from outside the tent, and only a few possessions were hidden. The bodies were left where they had been killed. A strong suspect was brought to trial in both cases, though not without significant evidence that both were innocent of the crimes for which they stood accused.

Elli Immo, meanwhile, was murdered while walking home in 1955. The theory has been proposed that Assmann had danced with the victim on the night before her death. Vieno Assmann was delighted to claim that her ex-husband was in Kemi that same evening.

Much of what is said about the German, including his own words, seems nowhere near reality. For example, he said on his deathbed that "I remember how Minister Penna Tervo cast a decisive vote in the presidential election and died two weeks later." Paloaro took that to mean he has assassinated the former Minister of Trade and Industry who died in a car crash in 1956 with no suspicious circumstances.

Assmann's sister has gone on record to say he received a pension from the Luftwaffe, meaning he was never in the SS or at Auschwitz. For the Saari murder, he appears to have actually been in Sweden. For other murders, he was known to be in Germany.

Key to the claims of the books and belief in Assmann as a uber-villain are the statements of his ex-wife. Vieno Assmann has been happy to provide "evidence" that her former husband was always in the area when a murder was committed. She equally claimed that he had incriminated himself in other ways, such as leaving the house with a shovel after the death of Kyllikki Saari. For a supposed KGB agent, he seemed very sloppy.

Many of these facts "confirmed" by his ex-wife need to be taken in the context that he was known to be a domestic abuser and adulterer. Assmann was arrested in 1961 for a brutal assault in public, and they were divorced in 1970. Yet, all these things are often ignored by those wishing to push the movie script suspect over the more mundane.

However, that isn't to say that nothing is alarming about Hans Assmann, and his story isn't without points of interest. In 1963, he was questioned over the murder of Sirkka-Liisa Valjus in Turku, Finland's oldest city. Valjus was a prostitute strangled using the power cord from a lamp.

Matti Paloaro and Jorma Palo's 2004 book *Trust or death! The Mystery of Hans Assmann* revealed that Assmann had been known to the victim.

"According to witnesses, Sirkka-Liisa Valjus had been accompanied on the night before the murder by a German, Finnish-speaking, and easily angered man. The taxi driver had believed her companion to be a German or a Dutchman and celebrated the New Year in Turku with him and Sirkka-Liisa. Turku residents also knew Hans had visited Sirkka-Liisa, and some had also seen his Opel."

Being questioned over both the Lake Bodom and Sirkka-Liisa Valjus murders is undoubtedly suggestive, yet once again, Assmann had an alibi for the murder.

While being questioned over the Valjus killing, police also allegedly asked him about murders in Sweden, such as the March 1958 killing of Agnetta Nyholm in Stockholm and the April 1958 murder of Birgitta Lövqvist at Västerbacken. They also inquired about the summer 1960 killings of Ulla Persson and Berit Lindqvist, both at Sundbyberg. Assmann had lived in both Västerbacken and Sundbyberg.

There was no evidence to link Assmann to any of them, and the serial killer John Ingvar Lövgren was later found guilty of murdering Agnetta Nyholm alongside three other women.

While the claims around Assmann may occasionally have a ring of truth, most of what he said was complete and utter fantasy and attempts to put a square peg into a round hole. He was a violent man, a war veteran, and an alcoholic; it is certainly possible that he may have been responsible for a serious crime, possibly even one or more of the many murders attributed to him. However, in many cases, the evidence is usually "found" by writers and enthusiasts to ensure Assmann is included, his name drawing immediate interest. There are even some online who suspect his involvement in killing John F. Kennedy, pointing out that Lee Harvey Oswald visited Helsinki in 1959. The Finnish police, meanwhile, consider the books written about him to be little more than fiction.

Hans Assmann may be the exciting supervillain everyone would like to have committed all the killings, yet the reality is that he simply isn't. It makes a great story, yet also it allows us to detach ourselves from reality. It is comforting to think that so many senseless and brutal murders are the work of one man and shadowy forces such as the KGB or an ex-Nazi. They are detached from us; they are not our friends or neighbors. The reality is, that's exactly who most murderers are, and all the killings attributed to Assmann were truthfully brutal, vicious, and sordid snapshots of our own human nature, not the work of a pantomime villain.

4 THE DISAPPEARANCE AND MURDER OF KYLLIKKI SAARI

Finland, 1953

Like the rest of Europe and the other Nordic countries, Finland was still recovering from the Second World War as Finns entered the 1950s. Life was more challenging than it once was. Yet, Finland was also undergoing the developments that we see today, opening up to closer integration with its Nordic cousins with the creation of the Nordic Council in 1952, with Finland joining in 1955. There was freedom of movement and other benefits that allowed Finland's economy to skyrocket, and fears of the Soviet Union were beginning to dissipate as the country looked toward joining the UN and moving West.

However, for all the progress that seemingly came daily, Finland was still traditionally rustic in many places, with most devoted to God and the rural positions that their ancestors had held for generations. Talk of international treaties, the Cold War, or even the likes of rock and roll will have had little airing here. One such person was Kyllikki Saari, a 17-year-old girl who lived in the isolated village of Möykky, traditional in her outlook, and innocent of the many horrors in the world.

It was May 17, 1953, and it was a Sunday. Kyllikki had attended church and later in the day would be returning to the town of Isojoki in Merikarvia for a Christian youth event, perhaps connected to Whitsun, which would be the week afterward on May 24. She was happy to attend, having many friends there, but told her parents that she didn't like the trip back between Isojoki and Möykky, finding the remote and forested road frightening, particularly in the dark. During the last winter, Kyllikki had been skiing alone through the forest close by and been scared by somebody so much that she skied to the nearest house, desperately phoning home and tearfully begging her father to come and pick her up.

The church meeting ended at 10pm, and Kyllikki had some solace in that her friend Maiju would be cycling part of the way with her. Unfortunately, the two had to depart with over 3 miles left to go, Maiju taking one path at a crossroads and Kyllikki taking another. Nervously, she said her goodbyes. Kyllikki wasn't naturally timid or nervous. In what was considered a safe and crime-free area, her concern over the road was marked as curious, some speculating that it had been a particular person she was concerned about, rather than more general anxiety.

She was right to be nervous. She didn't return home that night, nor on Monday. Kyllikki's parents weren't immediately worried as she had occasionally stayed over at Maiju's house without giving them notice beforehand. However, on Tuesday, the family received a call from the parish office inquiring why their daughter hadn't arrived for work. It now became clear that something was amiss, the police being contacted soon afterward.

The area was close-knit and, like most rural areas, very open to gossip. The news of the disappearance traveled quickly and throughout the region, with witnesses not being hard to find or unwilling to talk. A local laborer named Tie-Jaska was the first to come forward, saying he had seen the missing girl on Sunday around 10:40pm as she passed him on her bicycle. Another potential witness said they had seen a cream-colored car on the track and said it had a bike with it. Two other men followed, informing police that they had found a suspicious scene while driving a carriage on Monday, not far from the place that Jaska reported seeing Kyllikki. They said that there were footprints and tire marks on the dirt road's surface, with broken glass and signs of a struggle.

It would be two months before there was any significant break in the case, two people out picking summer berries spotting the handlebars of a bicycle sticking out of a bog. The wetland was hundreds of yards away from the dirt track that Kyllikki had been traveling on, but police quickly confirmed that the bike was hers. Despite the best hopes of locals and the authorities, it now became certain that they were dealing with a crime.

Kyllikki Saari. Public domain.

Whoever had thrown the bicycle into the bog had shown some level of intelligence, emptying the tires of air and twisting the handlebars so that it sank quicker. Intriguingly, the swamp had already been searched with a metal detector back in May, and the leather of the saddle was still in good condition, meaning that it had only been put there recently. The location of the find suggested somebody local had been involved.

Despite a thorough search, nothing new came up, and it wouldn't be until October, with winter drawing in, that the worst fears were confirmed. With the area about to be blanketed with heavy snow, police ordered a new site search to ensure nothing was missed on the ground. Searching the bog on October 10, police came across a bundle identified as one of Kyllikki s shoes. Inside the shoe were her scarf and a man's sock tied up with string. There were bite marks on the scarf, and it appeared to have been used as a gag, Kyllikki desperately trying to bite through it and call for help. The second shoe wasn't far away, and once again, they hadn't been there back in May.

Continuing the search on October 11 and undoubtedly knowing it was a hunt for a body, one of the searchers observed a tree branch sticking up from the bog a few hundred yards from the dirt road. Calling for assistance, the man and his friend pulled the wood from the wetland, observing that it was sharpened into a stake. It also smelled strongly of decomposition. The killer had used the stake to mark where he had dumped Kyllikki Saari's body.

Police investigators cordoned off the area and began the unpleasant and challenging task of securing the crime scene and extracting the corpse. As with the concealment of the bicycle, the grave showed cunning. The killer had made incisions on three sides to create a door of earth that could be lifted and replaced to show minimal signs of digging. Underneath the swampy hatch, the killer had dug down half a meter to bury the body. Investigators ascertained that the digger had been left-handed.

Searchers remove the body from the bog. Public domain.

Kyllikki was partially decomposed, her head and upper body being covered with her own jacket. One of her breasts had been taken out of her bra, and she was naked from the waist down. The state of decomposition meant that it was impossible to tell if Kyllikki had been in a struggle, as indicated by the evidence on the dirt track. While the partial nudity is suggestive, experts couldn't say for sure that she had been raped. However, they could tell that she certainly wasn't pregnant, cutting out the scurrilous gossip about the vicar. Again, the cause of death wasn't certain, but there was significant damage to the head and face, with a broken nose and two broken cheekbones, seemingly done with a heavy weapon such as a rock.

The coroner also ascertained that the stick used to mark the grave had pierced Kyllikki's stomach and had been thrust down into the corpse months after her death. This perhaps suggests that the killer had wanted the body to be found by making it obvious to the search party. With his deliberate, methodical, and intelligent hiding of the bicycle and corpse, it seems odd that he would otherwise have left such an obvious sign to be discovered. The covering of Kyllikki's face with her jacket is also telling, with murderers who do so often being emotionally connected with the victim or remorseful for their actions, being unable to look upon their work.

A criminal profile produced after the killing said that the culprit would be over 30 years old in age and would live alone. He had few social connections and may have been pointed out as exhibiting unusual behavior by others in the community. He would be local, have planned the crime meticulously, and possibly may have known the victim. However, it was uncertain whether it was a deliberately targeted killing, and he may have taken an opportunity when running into her on the dirt road. His skill at hiding the body and evidence suggested he had criminal experience and may have killed before. Given how involved the locals were in the hunt for Kyllikki, it seems possible he may have joined the search teams to avoid suspicion.

Despite the lengths the killer went to hide his identity, there was no shortage of suspects in the case. The most publicly prominent was the aforementioned parish priest, Kauko Kanervo. Kanervo had moved to a new parish just weeks before the disappearance, and Kyllikki had written a letter to him on religious matters. How the rumor that she was pregnant by him began isn't known, and even though it was proven false, the allegations of impropriety persisted and would eventually be proven correct.

Kanervo was a sexual predator who targeted young girls, particularly teenagers, and had particularly requested that Kyllikki work with him at his pastor's office. While he initially denied all knowledge of anything untoward, three years later, police received a report that he had sexually molested a 16-year-old. Under questioning, Kanervo admitted that he had asked Kyllikki to masturbate him. He also admitted having sexual relations with his maid and his sister and being sent home from missionary work in Africa for inappropriateness toward women there.

However, Kanervo's sexual liaisons may also have been his savior as the maid gave him a strong alibi for the night that Kyllikki went missing — she was in bed with him at the time. His 9-year-old daughter confirmed he was at home in Merikarvia, and there were only 20 minutes of his night unaccounted for. Being unable to drive and the distance being 40 miles in any case, he was discounted from inquiries.

While the evidence against Pastor Kanervo in the Kyllikki case was almost exclusively rumor and innuendo, that against Vihtori Lehmusviita was anything but. Lehmusviita was a dangerous man, having been found guilty of sexual offenses in the

1940s and found to be mentally ill. By now 38-years-old, he worked odd jobs around Isojoki, being engaged in ditch digging at the time.

Lehmusviita lived within a mile of the crime scene and kept a common working field with his brother-in-law just 165 feet from where the body of Kyllikki Sarri was found. Indeed, police suspected a shovel found in the field was the one used to dig the grave.

The suspect was an alcoholic, and police believed he'd had assistance in the crime from his brother-in-law. The two allegedly attempted to cover up Lehmusviita's actions alongside his mother, who gave him an alibi, saying her son had been asleep by 7pm as he was heavily intoxicated. Pulled in for questioning before discovering the body, Lehmusviita said that Sarri was dead and her body would never be found. He later recanted his words, saying that he hadn't known what he was saying.

Despite the circumstantial evidence, there wasn't enough for police to make an arrest, and after the interrogation, he was committed to a mental institution. His brother-in-law moved to the Central Ostrobothnia region of the country and then emigrated to Sweden.

While Lehmusviita may seem like a strong suspect, much rests on his being in the right location and the right time, with his statement needing to be taken in the context of mental illness and alcoholism. Despite his record, locals couldn't believe he was involved, and like with Kanervo, the evidence was weak.

In the end, nobody was charged. In all, police interviewed 5000 different individuals and had nearly 400 separate lines of inquiry, all coming to nothing. The case became one of the most infamous in Finland's history, generating the perfect storm of innocence, brutality, and scandal.

Was Kyllikki Saari a victim of a Cold War accident as those pushing the Hans Assmann theory would have us believe, or was it an opportunistic serial killer? Was she deliberately targeted? Or, did she simply come across evil coming her way one night in that dark forest? We are unlikely to ever know. However, Saari wouldn't be the only girl mysteriously killed around this time in Finland...

5 THE CHRISTMAS KILLING OF ELLI IMMO

Finland, 1955

Lapland is seen as a magical place. A land where the snow often falls to a depth of over a meter, and sleds cross picturesque scenes full of fir trees, lights, and Santa Claus for the tourists. It's a place of rustic charm where nothing evil could ever happen… Sadly, perception and reality are not the same things, and Lapland has just as many issues as anywhere else in the world. Life is hard, and while the cold may seem remarkable to tourists staying a matter of days, the Baltic winds chill locals to the bone. *Game of Thrones'* famous warning of "winter is coming" could almost be made for this one area of Finland.

Such was the winter of 1955. In the city of Kemi, southern Lapland, three young women stood freezing in the night air. Maila, Anna Liisa and Elli, more fully

Elli Maria Immo. The three had looked around the sights and done a copious amount of window shopping, with the city getting ready for Christmas. It was December 7, and perhaps there were wooden toys for children in the windows, maybe new clothes or food displayed for passing shoppers.

As the clock struck 9pm, Maila told her friends that her feet were freezing and it was time to go home. The three separated, with Maila and Elli, headed one way and Anna Liisa the other. The two friends lived close to each other and, already pitch black, it was safer to walk in pairs. While crime was not an issue, there were numerous dangers, from snow, ice, or even wild animals. However, there was something far more dangerous than a wolf stalking its prey in Kemi that night.

Elli Immo was born on August 10, 1935 in Alatornio. Her father was a police officer there, and after his unexpected death, the family moved to Kemi. She enjoyed her time in the 25,000 strong city, significant for the area, being friendly, cheerful, and sociable. The family lived in the suburbs, and in the fall of 1954, Elli enrolled at the Kemi School of Economics alongside having a part-time job as a business assistant in the wallpaper and paint trade. She was a typical student that we would recognize today, being more concerned with her life in the city center, going dancing, watching movies, and spending time with friends at cafes. She was having fun.

On December 6, Elli had enjoyed an entertaining night when she traveled around 5 miles to Lautiosaari. An early Christmas party was underway at the

Karelian Society House, and she had tickets. There was dancing and plenty of men. Elli had attracted the particular attention of one man, yet it didn't seem unwelcome as the following day she expressed how much fun she'd had to her friends.

The morning of December 7, however, had been unusual for her. Elli hadn't seemed her usual jovial self, and witnesses described her as sullen or even angry. It transpired that she had quarreled with another student over photographs. Yet, it wasn't as trivial as it initially sounded. A boy at the Kemi School of Economics was tasked with collecting class photo orders and subscriptions. However, nobody knew that the photo studio being used offered a 10% discount for all students. The boy was pocketing the extra money for himself, and Elli exposed the fraud. Brought before the Students' Union, they decided the extra money should go to them. The boy was outraged and had written Elli a letter that police later described as "malicious."

However, all was forgotten by the evening, and she set out on the town with Maila and Anna Liisa. They headed to the three cinemas in the city and tried to find a movie; however, Elli and Anna Liisa had already seen what Maila wanted to watch.

Instead, they went to the Mokka-Tuva café and then Valio Bar before heading home. As Malia and Elli set off, two young teenage boys asked to escort them but were turned down. Pulling their beanie hats tight to keep out the cold, the two went along the Lapintie Road. Elli had crocheted her hat herself and was said to be very proud of it. Arriving at Elli's house, Malia asked if she minded walking a little way with her toward her home, there being no street lights at all. Elli didn't mind and joined her friend for around 275 yards of the journey. The two parted around 9:30pm, and Elli began the short distance back home. She would never make it.

Before midnight, Elli's mother returned from work, walking the same path her daughter would have walked. The front door was unlocked, but this was usual, with fear of crime being almost nonexistent. Elli's three brothers were already asleep, and the rooms were hot, Elli having warmed the house as usual when she had got home from classes. The girl's bags and books were still present on the living room floor, and her mother deduced she must have done some study before heading out. Her absence wasn't particularly worrying as her daughter had been known to spend the night at Anna-Liisa's before. Though, she usually took some bedding with her…

At 12:50pm the following day, a schoolboy discovered Elli Immo's body lying on her stomach next to the path from Lapintie to Ristikanka, where she lived. She was just 100 feet from home. She was wearing the same dark green jacket and winter boots as the night before, and her beloved crocheted grey beanie had fallen beside her. She was covered in snow. Her killer had struck brutally, stabbing her several times in the right side of the neck and behind the ear, the cause of death. Some of the snow had been placed there by her killer, covering her face and upper body. Despite the corpse laying on a public path, including the one that Elli's own mother had walked, the body had been somehow undiscovered.

Elli Immo. Public domain.

Investigating the scene, police noted footprints from a large man's ski boot and bicycle tracks in the snow. Next to the body was found the sheath for a Mora knife. Morakniv knives have been crafted in Östnor, Sweden, for over a century. They were standard for many craftsmen, once being handmade by generation after generation. Alongside crafts, they are frequently used for the likes of camping and bushcraft. Owning one in Lapland would not be unusual. The murder weapon was never found by police, though a knife was handed in after it was found on a bus, police being unable to ascertain whether it was connected to the killing.

Police carried out extensive inquiries and searches in Kemi, with 60 people quickly questioned, including Maila, who said she had gone home and listened to the radio. Police checked with the broadcaster to ensure that the programs began when she said they did. In today's age of ready information, it seems rather strange that such a thing could be a legitimate alibi. Still, we must remember the era and the community's isolation, where radio schedules were unavailable and frequently prone to interruption. Speaking with a 22-year-old who lodged at Elli's home meanwhile, the young woman recanted that the previous evening she'd heard a loud shout followed by a quieter exclamation between 9.45pm and 9:50pm. It had sounded like somebody in need.

The photo scam boy was questioned, but an alibi placed him at home all night, with family testifying on his behalf.

Elli was neither robbed nor sexually assaulted, leading police to theorize she had either been the victim of a lunatic or her father's police work had been the motive, someone from his past seeking revenge. Her father was strait-laced and strict, formerly working the western border and stopping smuggling. Though why somebody might target Elli when her father was long dead was never made clear, and the sense that police were struggling for either a motive or a suspect was apparent.

A truck driver was arrested, with his clothes being sent for analysis. Although oily from his profession, no concrete evidence was found against him, and he was released. Clothes were taken from others, homes searched, knives analyzed. Witnesses reported a strange man who jumped off a train mid-journey; another said a man was conducting his own personal inquiry. The police file was full of false reports and rumors.

The only suspect who has ever been named as having been questioned is Runar Holmström. He is the suspect brought to trial for the double murder of two young women during the infamous Tulilahti campsite murders, which we will deal with more fully in the next chapter.

Holmström, a petty thief, stood accused of the stabbing and bludgeoning of Riitta Pakkanen, 23, and Eine Nyyssönen, 21, having admitted to stalking the girls on his moped. The bodies were dragged from their tent in the middle of the night in July 1959, being buried in a grave at a nearby swamp. However, there was significant evidence that Holmström was innocent, a belief publicly stated by both the prosecutor and judge after his suicide in 1961.

However, on February 22, 1960, Central Criminal Police interrogated Holmström over Elli Immo. He denied the murder and said that he was at home in Munsala through the entire winter of 1955–1956. However, in many respects, he was evasive. When asked where he acquired the Mora knife he carried, Holmström could only say he had received it "somehow" in September 1959, yet couldn't explain where. The sheath that he put the knife in wasn't the original one that came with it, and again, Holmström couldn't remember what happened to the original. When asked whether anyone except those in his household could verify he'd been at home, he said that guests had come over but couldn't name who. He refused to give a handwriting sample, even though that would have little bearing on the case.

Eventually, nothing came of the investigation, and the case went cold. However, in 1972, two of the original three Kemi Police Department officers on the matter, Juho Tepponen, and Pekka Vitikka, stated that the affair should be reinvestigated, saying that the perpetrators had been protected during the original 1955 inquiries. However, despite their statements, they never made a formal request for an investigation into the allegation. Some thought that a police officer had been involved in the killing.

The murder of Elli Immo is one of those tragic crimes with no motive, no suspect, and very little chance of a resolution. Police were at a loss in 1955, and today the case is long since cold. The hope that somebody in old age might yet be brought to justice is very slim. While Runar Holmström may have been alarming in some of his statements, there was nothing to really link him with the crime, and Hans Assmann should probably be dismissed as the fiction that the police claim his crimes to be. With all suspects eliminated, it seems justice for Elli Immo will remain forever elusive.

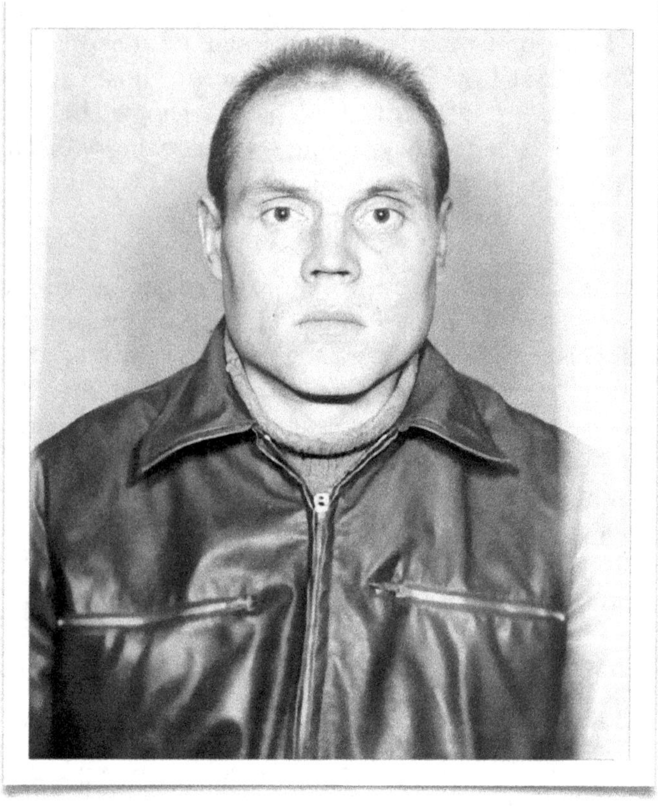

Runar Holmström mugshot.
Holmström is a suspect in the Elli Immo and Tulilahti campsite cases. Police photo.

6 THE DOUBLE MURDER AT THE TULILAHTI CAMPSITE

Finland 1959

Everyone enjoys summer vacation. It's supposed to be a time of relaxation and enjoyment, a time away from the daily trials of work and life's general stress. There are always problems, however. Perhaps there might be issues with tickets, hotel rooms, or something as trivial as not enough chairs at the swimming pool. Rarely do such vacations turn to murder. Yet, in 1959, that's precisely what happened to two young women in Finland. Their deaths became one of the most infamous unsolved cases in the country's history.

It was July 18, 1959, and office worker Riitta Aulikki Pakkanen, 23, and nursing student Eine Maria Nyyssönen, 21, had long since decided they would go on a bicycle trip from their home in Jyväskylä to Savo and North Karelia. They had been anticipating the excursion for months, building up their fitness and going on long practice rides. It was very much a makeshift trip, with Riitta borrowing a camera from her brother and both women sewing their own bags to carry belongings.

Eine Nyyssönen. Public domain.

The summer was a beautiful one, and over the first week, they had spent a night at the Naarajärvi camping area and then been haymaking in Rantasalmi. They continued from a campsite in Punkaharju, onward towards Savonlinna, boarding a ship to Joensuu.

"Wonderful!!! We have been here for one night and this wonderful morning," Eine wrote home to her mother from Savonlinna. "The shore of Lake Pielisjärvi has been the most beautiful thing on this trip…."

By July 25, the pair had reached Koli, a village at the foot of Koli Hill beside the picturesque Lake Pielinen, the area being a national park and a place of stunning natural beauty. Sending a postcard home, Eine said that the women intended to visit the town of Varkaus and be home by July 30. Riding through the country in Panama hats and cotton blouses, they likely turned many heads, and as the sun shone, they must have felt like they didn't have a care in the world.

However, when the two hadn't returned by August 3 and Riitta hadn't shown up for work, the alarm was raised, and missing person reports were filed. Eine Nyyssönen was 5'3" with a slender frame, full face, dark brown curly hair, and blue-green eyes. She was softly spoken and walked briskly. Riitta Pakkanen was the same height and had blond hair. Her eyes were described as blue-gray, her face oval, and her manner calm. Both lived at home with their parents and had positive relationships with their families.

Police quickly ascertained that the last known sighting had been from July 27, when they had stayed at a hostel before moving on. Presuming they intended to make for Varkaus as mentioned on the postcard, the search started there. At this point, police are said to have suspected that the pair had suffered an accident, likely drowning.

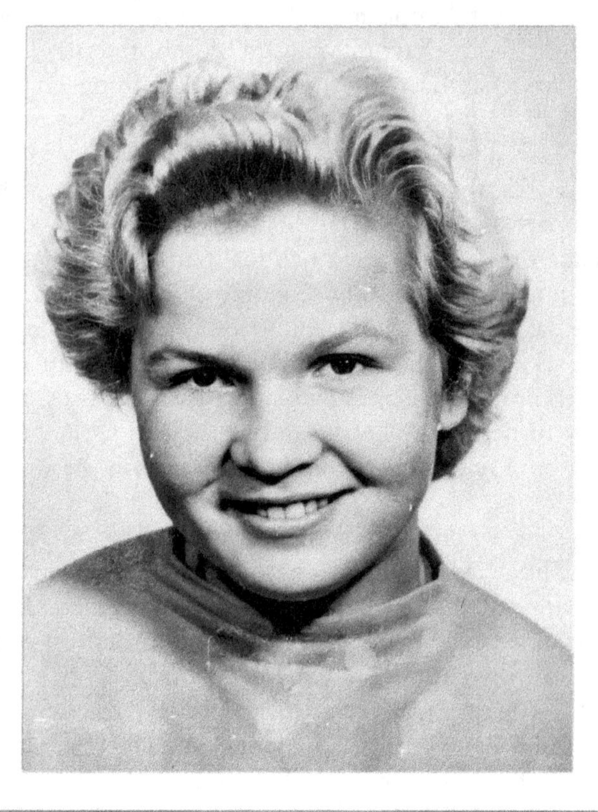

Riitta Pakkanen. Public domain.

Varkaus didn't bring results, however, and the trail went cold, with few leads on where the women may have gone. Their parents made the trip to help in the search, and the Finnish Air Force was tasked with flying over the area, producing aerial photos to locate any sign of the missing women. Still, there was nothing found. Six days after police were alerted to the disappearance, two local men, Keijo and Heikki, heard the news on the radio. They approached the authorities to tell them they had spent time with the girls at a local campsite, giving statements of what they remember from the night in question.

With a new search window open, police and locals scoured the area for any sign of Riitta and Eine. Divers searched the bottom of the lake for over a hundred yards, but still, there was nothing. However, on August 21, a soldier assisting the search found their bodies in a bog close to Tulilahti campsite in Heinävesi, a 40-minute drive from Varkaus.

Riitta had been killed with a heavy blow to the skull, while Eine had been stabbed and was found undressed. There was, however, no evidence she had been raped. The killer or killers had then gone to some length to cover up the crime, with the grave being 220 yards from camp. Both bodies had been placed in the swamp where the killer had dug a hole that night, ten feet long and 10 inches deep. The hole was covered over by several thick logs and large pieces of peat, and it's likely that the murderer would have gone deeper had he not hit a long fallen branch. Another branch was used to cover the scene to make it less apparent that there had been a disturbance.

Inside the grave, Eine's face had been covered by a black anorak, and other clothing had been piled on top of the bodies, partially seemingly to hide Riitta's nudity. It is believed that she was naked when attacked rather than having been stripped by the killer. The victim's other belongings had been hidden carefully, with some of them found to be missing, including most of their money. On September 4, police found Riitta and Eine's bicycles in the deepest part of Tulilahti lake, proving the killer had used a boat, of which there were many around the shoreline.

Investigations at the site revealed that the two victims had arrived at the campground on July 27, pitching their own tent and spending time with two young local men who had come in a motorboat, the previously mentioned Keijo and Heikki. It wasn't believed they were known to each other beforehand. The campsite was in poor condition and small, being little over 165 by 65 feet. Felled trees from a recent storm littered the area, and there were no facilities. Keijo helped the women light a fire, allowing them to heat water. They drank cocoa and ate fins, offering the boys some of the cocoa, which they rejected, preferring coffee. The atmosphere was playful and light-hearted, the boys departing in good humor around 12:30am.

However, they hadn't been the only non-campers near the site. Both earlier in the day and that night, witnesses described a man on a moped who they had observed acting suspiciously, seemingly stalking Riitta and Eine, driving behind them out of sight. He had been secretly watching the two young men and women all night. Other witnesses said they had seen a man lurking around the camp after sunset, entering the toilet.

Police ascertained that the murders had to have occurred that night or into the early morning as, by daybreak, the campsite was empty. Crime scene investigators established that the killer had cut the tent open to get inside and struck immediately, killing the girls right there. He stabbed Eine in the back, likely as she tried to flee, and then stabbed Riitta, finishing her off with blows to the head. It was a furious assault, speaking only of rage.

News of the killings spread quickly and was a sensation, thousands of people descending on the Tulilahti crime scene. The feeling was high in the area, with people openly threatening to lynch the murderer when apprehended.

Acting quickly, the first arrests were made, five local men. The press identified them as Reino, Lauri, and Martin from whose house the killer took the shovel. There was also a carpenter known to them, Teuvo, and a gravedigger, Ferdinand, on whose pasture the body was discovered. Next, they arrested Keijo and Heikki. All the detained had blood samples taken and had their clothes examined. The feeling that an under-pressure local police force was wildly hoping for a piece of luck is inescapable.

Ferdinand was released first after a thorough interrogation and search of his home. Meanwhile, Lauri gave an alibi of being at Teuvo's house, witnessed by the carpenter's mother. He claimed to have headed home to bed by 10pm. Meanwhile, Lauri's nephew, Reino, provided an alibi for Keijo and Heikki, saying he met them on the Tulilahti road, and they asked him to say hello to the girls, both seemingly leaving. Martin had no particular alibi but also said he was in bed and his mother was a witness.

Again with samples taken and clothes checked for blood, all three were released.

Teuvo, however, raised more interest when human blood was found on the lining of his jacket, seemingly having been washed out. There was blood on the back, shoulders, armpit, near the right turn of the collar, and at the mouth of the left breast pocket. Subsequent analysis found that it was type O, the same as Teuvo himself. The suspect could not explain how it got there but said that he injured his hand during a fishing trip when he accidentally smashed a bottle of alcohol. He added that he also hurt his hand with a nail during work on his house. Teuvo was released after four days.

Keijo and Heikki, meanwhile, told police about the man on the moped, having observed him themselves during their time at the camp with the two women. They identified the bike as a light blue Solifer with a brown briefcase on the luggage rack. Keijo, meanwhile, admitted that he had tried to make several passes at Riitta and Eine, trying to force a hug or kiss, all of which were rejected. Both were released.

With the locals eliminated from inquiries, police focused their attention on the mysterious moped rider. An appeal described him as "30–40 years old, medium-sized, dark-skinned" and described his moped as "bluish in color… similar to, for example, the Silver Wing, Husqvarna, Roulette, Rabenack or Solifer."

"As the identification of this man can have a very decisive effect on the investigation of the criminal case in question, the police seriously ask all persons who have seen such a man or who may otherwise provide some information about him to report immediately to the nearest police authorities."

Holmström arrives at his trial in irons. Public domain.

There was only ever one real suspect in the case, Runar Holmström, 37. Holmström, the son of an economist, was identified by witnesses as possibly the man seen on the moped. He was arrested in November, already wanted for numerous aggravated thefts. Upon investigations at his home, police found a knife that experts believed fit the cuts that had been made to the tree branch left over the grave. They also discovered a pistol that was loaded with the safety off, ready for use. When he was taken to the crime scene, police observed that he acted nervously. They believed they had their man.

Upon further questioning, Holmström admitted that he had been the man who was observed watching the girls, insisting he had continued on his journey to Varkaus at midnight. He also confessed other information that the police believed could only have been known by the killer, such as Keijo and Heikki trying to hug and kiss the girls.

Holmström withdrew his confession, but it was too late, and the admission only confirmed in the minds of investigators that he was guilty, despite the evidence only being circumstantial.

In fact, there was a lot of evidence that Holmström was innocent. For example, experts had ascertained that the killer would have been left-handed given how the tree branch was cut. Holmström was right-handed. He was only 5'4" tall, meaning that overpowering two women, carrying the bodies over rough terrain, and digging the grave would have been an arduous task, particularly over the few hours the crime appeared to have taken place in.

A police reconstruction proved that the murder, burial, and hiding of all the belongings could have been done in the time, but that was only with police knowing precisely what they were doing and where everything was, including the shovel taken from the farm of the previously arrested suspects. It seems likely that the only way it would have been possible for somebody to carry out the murders would be if the culprit or culprits had local knowledge and had preplanned the disposal of the bodies. Holmström lived over 25 miles away in the Western Ostrobothnia region.

In the spring of 1961, while Holmström was in prison awaiting trial, women's underwear and two Panama hats judged to belong to Riitta and Eine were found near Varkaus. The items still had color and had clearly been there no time at all. They were certainly not present during the last winter, and by this point, Holmström had been in prison for nearly a year and a half.

Despite the new evidence, the trial went ahead a few months later, beginning on June 8, 1960, and held at Hasumäki Primary School. However, it was never concluded as on May 8, 1961, Holmström hanged himself with a rope fashioned from the bedsheets in his cell. He had tried to commit suicide before using barbiturates prescribed for insomnia. On another occasion, his brother smuggled codeine into the prison inside a bible. However, it was discovered before being passed onto the suspect, and he was stopped in his attempt. While some may suggest his suicide showed a guilty conscience, it's worth noting that many prisoners at the time were frightened of the harsh punishments dealt out to the guilty, namely forced labor, where many were worked to death.

But if the culprit hadn't been Runar Holmström, then who? The locals were mentioned, of course, yet when police arrested Holmström, they ended other lines of inquiry, which has brought Principal Investigator Axel

Skogman much criticism over the years. Police concluding that the case was closed after Holmström's suicide has likewise been criticized, as has the failure to link the affair to Kyllikki Saari.

With Runar Holmström dying before the trial ended, there was no conclusion to the case. Yet, police believed the matter over, despite the prosecutor and judge being on record to say they thought the suspect was innocent. Whether Holmström actually was involved, the answers lay more locally, or even Hans Assmann may have been lurking in the shadows, we will never know. With over sixty years having passed, it seems that the double murder at the Tulilahti campsite will be yet another crime that goes unsolved.

7 THE SLAUGHTER AT LAKE BODOM

Finland, 1960

Finland is rich in unsolved and infamous crimes. There was the stove murder in Kokemäki, the disappearance of Hilkka Laitinen, the Helsinki cellar killings, and the notorious Viking Sally mystery, all of which will be covered in volume two of this book. However, the most infamous is possibly the shocking Lake Bodom murders, a crime that has enthralled Finland for over sixty years.

It was June 4, 1960, and despite the Cold War raging between the Soviet Union and Western powers, optimism would have been the outlook of many teenage Finns at the turn of the decade. They didn't remember the Second World War that had brought the nation such hardships and instead were more interested in Western stars such as Elvis Presley, The King having recently found a footing in the country.

Four such teenagers were Maila Irmeli Björklund and Anja Tuulikki Mäki, both 15, and their boyfriends Seppo Antero Boisman and Nils Wilhelm Gustafsson, both 18. All were from the city of Vantaa, not far from Helsinki.

Maila Björklund, Anja Mäki and Seppo Boisman. Public domain.

Seppo was the eldest of the group and was working to become an electrician while he waited for his impending mandated military service like Nils. His girlfriend, Anja, was the youngest, having turned 15 in April. The popular one of the group, Nils, was what they would have termed a greaser in the United States, never seen without his leather jacket. His girlfriend, Maila, would be celebrating her 16th birthday in just two days. The relationships were relatively new, with Seppo and Anja having been going out since the spring and Nils dating Maila for just three weeks.

The Saturday was a summer's day during a record heatwave, with Pentecost taking place that Sunday and celebrations planned for Pentecost Monday. The festival is much more significant in terms of public celebration in the Scandinavian countries. With time off work, the festival has coincided with several murders, this case being the first of three such incidents told in this book.

Our group of four wouldn't be thinking about anything as dark as that; however, when they decided to take a romantic camping trip to the shores of the nearby Lake Bodom in Espoo, 16 miles away. They took two motorcycles and set up their rough camp near a popular beach, planning on swimming, fishing, and staying the night. It would have been a relaxing and loved-up time, and all four were seemingly asleep by midnight. Whether deliberate, through discomfort or simple excitement, the four woke around 2am and the boys went fishing again, the girls falling back to sleep.

Around 6am, a group of birdwatching boys noticed that the group's tent had collapsed, and a blond man was apparently witnessed by a short-sighted boy walking away from the campsite. However, they dismissed the scene, and it wouldn't be until 11am that the true horror of what had happened at Lake Bodom became apparent when a carpenter named Esko Oiva Johansson came across a scene of carnage, alerting the police. Maila Björklund, Anja Mäki and Seppo Boisman were all dead.

In the early hours of June 5, sometime between 4am and 6am, an unknown assailant had approached the group's tent from outside and cut the ropes, causing it to collapse. They had repeatedly stabbed through the material with a knife, also using an unidentified blunt instrument to bludgeon those inside. Police suspected it was a rock, and both weapons were never found.

At the scene, a partially nude Maila was dead on top of the ruined tent, with an alive Nils lying next to her. She had suffered the most extensive injuries of anyone, stabbed 15 times, including after death, showing a fit of uncontrolled anger. There were defensive wounds to her arms. Nils, meanwhile, had suffered a fractured jaw, concussion, and broken facial bones. A slash to his cheek was so deep that his teeth could be seen, and he was leaking cerebral fluid through his nose. Without urgent care, he would almost certainly have died. Seppo had also been stabbed, and all had blunt force trauma.

Police investigate damage to the tent. Police photo.

Alongside the killing, the assailant had taken several items, including the group's motorcycle keys. While that would have made logical sense beforehand to ensure nobody escaped, it made little sense afterward, mainly as the killer hadn't seemingly had an opportunity to enter the tent. Unless, of course, the killings had been preplanned. Meanwhile, Seppo's and Nils' shoes were hidden around 550 yards from the camp beside a road, and Seppo's leather jacket was also missing.

What was found at the scene was almost as intriguing as what was not. A pillowcase was found tied with an elastic band. Blood and semen were found on the material, and the blood was undeterminable, possibly being a mixture of several individuals. The semen, meanwhile, didn't match either of the boys.

Police severely hampered their own investigation by failing to secure the crime scene. The camp was not cordoned off, and no descriptions were taken. Police officers crowded the site and trampled all over the evidence, leaving much of it disturbed. They even allowed a party of soldiers to assist with searching for missing items, only adding to the number of bodies filling the area.

The public was outraged at the killings, with opinion running high just as it had been the year before after the Tulilahti campsite killings when two women were murdered. The suspect in those murders, Runar Holmström, was already under lock and key, with many believing he was innocent. With the pressure on and nobody by way of a suspect, police consulted a hypnotist.

Both Nils Gustafsson and the short-sighted witness

were put under hypnosis to create a picture of the assailant. Nils managed to remember that the man he had apparently seen was blond, claiming that the weapon he was wielding was a lead pipe. Such raises the possibility that the pillowcase had been used to wrap the blunt instrument to not leave fingerprints, which wouldn't explain the semen, however.

The sketch produced from little information was striking, yet also concerning, being built from the recollections of somebody who admitted to poor eyesight and somebody obscured by a tent and under attack. However, it bore an astonishing likeness to one man: Hans Assmann.

We have explored the theories surrounding Assmann at length already in this book. Still, as the Lake Bodom killings were one of the two crimes featured here that he was questioned about in his lifetime, we will briefly recap his involvement.

After emigrating to Finland, Assmann lived in the nearby village of Bodom, and his behavior at Helsinki Surgical Hospital on June 6 was marked out as unusual and alarming by Professor Jorma Palo. Assmann had arrived at the medical facility covered in red stains that appeared to be blood, with dirty fingernails, and was believed by some to have been faking unconsciousness. He was said to have been aggressive and nervous during his entire stay. Palo was confident he was the killer, and after the publication of the sketch, he cut his blond hair short.

Palo would write several books about Assmann, and in 1997, on his deathbed, he would tell his life story to former police officer and then editor of the *Alibi* true crime magazine, Matti Paloaro.

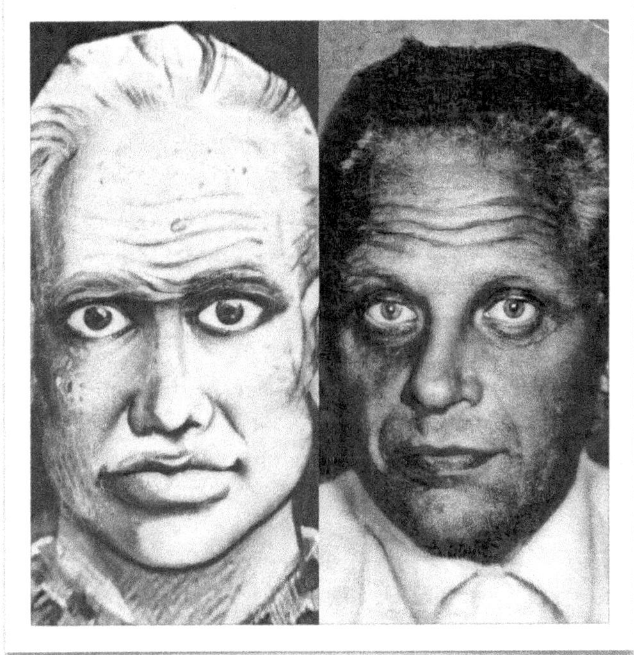

Police sketch comparison with Assmann.

As far as Bodom went, Assmann would offer vague hints, as with much of what he said. Following the publication of the books, it was proven that much of his alleged criminality was impossible and the work of a fantasist or fraudster. The police believe that the allegations are entirely fictional.

"I suppose you expect me to tell about those tent and knife things...." Assmann told Paloaro. "I have to disappoint you; I will not speak about the details; I will not admit nor deny things."

Assmann had a solid alibi for the time of the Lake Bodom murders as he had been cheating on his wife at the time and spent the entire night with his lover. The pair weren't alone in the house at any point, and the others present confirmed that he could not have left the building without them seeing him do so. Assmann never went anywhere. While the incident at the hospital was seemingly never explained, at least not publicly, police never considered Assmann a serious suspect in the Lake Bodom carnage.

While dismissing Assmann, police at the time of the murders did have another suspect, a kiosk keeper named Valdemar Gyllström, his kiosk being very close to the crime scene.

Gyllström was the prime suspect locally and known to have been previously belligerent toward campers, cutting down tents, throwing rocks at people in the street, firing a shotgun at people on a moped, and even hiding razor blades in apples to stop children stealing them. Gyllström had been mentally ill ever since the Second World War and had once been institutionalized; he was also an alcoholic who abused his wife and children. He had reportedly confessed to the killings to several people in the Oittaa district on the southern shore of Lake Bodom. Also, Gyllström had ensured that a local well was filled in soon after the massacre, a fact that locals believe had been done to conceal evidence. Those people even included his own son-in-law. Some later said that they had seen

Gyllström walking away from the crime scene but were too afraid of him to approach the authorities.

Police searches of his house turned up nothing incriminating, and he also had a solid alibi for the morning of the killings, having been at home with his wife. Gyllström was dismissed from the inquiry and died in 1969 via drowning in what may have been a suicide. Afterward, on her deathbed, his wife revealed she had been forced to give the alibi.

In 2016, local politician and Espoo resident Ulf Johansson wrote *The Legend of Bodom*, which fingered Gyllström for the killings. Johansson said that the group being from Vantaa was important, as no locals would have dared camp at the site through their fear of Gyllström.

"The kiosk man held the village in the grip of terror," Johansson told the Finnish Broadcasting Company. "The risk of reprisals was considered great; they wanted to protect themselves and their children."

"In fact, the Bodom murders were never a mystery to the locals," wrote Johansson in his book. "From the beginning, both the Espoo police and the residents of the area have been sure of who the Bodom killer is. But he was never convicted; his confession came too late."

However, the most intriguing piece of evidence from Johansson was the telling of how exactly Gyllström died. Speaking with a friend from the time, Börje, Johansson revealed that hours before his death, Gyllström had confessed again, telling his friend that he had carried out the killings. Distressed, Gyllström asked Börje what he should do, with Börje telling him, "If it is you who has done it, I think you should drown yourself, because you will spend the rest of your life in prison." Whether this indicates his guilt or that a mentally ill man was essentially directed to his suicide is open to interpretation.

The case went cold with no other suspects of note, seemingly destined to be yet another unsolved set of murders. Decades went by, and undoubtedly the culprit felt safe and secure that he had got away with possibly the most notorious crime in Finnish history. Ten years. Twenty. And then thirty. Then forty. That was until 2004 when police arrested Nils Gustafsson.

Investigators had used new technology to reanalyze blood evidence from the crime scene and concluded that Nils, then aged 62, had, in fact, been the killer all along. Police stated that they had always suspected as much.

Brought to trial in August 2005, the prosecution alleged that Nils Gustafsson, now a bus driver, had been drunk and attempted to initiate sex with Maila, being denied. He was turned out of the tent after getting into a fight with Seppo that ended with Nils' jaw being broken.

New DNA analysis on Nils Gustafsson's shoes revealed that only the blood of Maila, Anja, and Seppo was present, meaning they were likely hidden before any injury was suffered by Nils, according to the prosecution. If the hiding of the shoes happened after the killings but before the injury to Nils, then logic dictated that Nils must be the killer, having carried out the slaughter, hidden the items, and then returned to the scene to stage his own injuries and unconsciousness.

Nils Gustafsson. Public domain.

As a witness, the prosecution presented the former

lead detective on the case, who told the courtroom that during interrogations back in 1960, Nils had said, "What is done is done. I'll get 15 years for it".

However, the comment was never recorded and can be interpreted either as an expression of guilt or one of foreboding, with the young man fearing he would be wrongly implicated in the crime. A second witness stated that on the night of the murder, Nils and Seppo joined her on the shore. Nils was trying to start a fight with his friend, she alleged.

Yet, while Nils Gustafsson may seem like a good fit for the crime, questions remained unanswered. As the defense asked, would it really have been possible for Nils to inflict his own injuries? They were so severe, remember, that brain fluid was leaking from his nose, and he suffered a cut so deep to his face that his teeth were visible through his cheek. And if they were self-inflicted, how did Nils hide the weapon used while suffering from them? He had suffered such an extensive injury that it took several weeks of recovery and was seen by numerous doctors, none of who raised the alarm. Equally, what happened to the other missing items, such as the leather jacket? The killings, the defense argued, must have been the work of one or more people outside of the group.

On October 7, 2005, Nils Gustafsson was found not guilty on all charges. The prosecution's evidence was said to have been inconclusive, the motive proposed was not proportionate to the severity of the crime, and many facts were now impossible to ascertain given the length of time that had passed on the case.

The Finnish state paid him €44,900 for mental suffering.

With 61 years having passed, it seems unlikely that a suspect will ever be found guilty of the massacre at Lake Bodom. Gyllström and Assmann are long dead, and Nils Gustafsson is now approaching 80 years of age. Whether any of them were responsible or none of them, the killings were shocking in their brutality and have enthralled a nation ever since, inspiring books, TV, and even a horror movie. Yet, this was no script, and the evil walking at Lake Bodom that night was not a ghoul, fiend, or creature of our imagination. The killer was all too human, and that may be the most frightening horror of all.

8 THE SLAYING OF SIRKKA-LIISA VALJUS

Finland, 1963

Finland during the 1950s and 1960s was the scene of some shocking and truly monstrous incidents, and it must have seemed that the country was a haven for murders to get away with their crimes. Cases we've already talked about such as Kyllikki Saari, the Tulilahti campsite killings, and the Lake Bodom massacre have generated many comments and theories. At the same time, the brutal murder of Elli Immo, for example, remains relatively obscure. So too does the murder of Sirkka-Liisa Valjus, and just like the reporting on Western crime, it's hard to escape the feeling that class and the victim's character play a part in that.

Sirkka-Liisa Valjus, 34, was a woman who liked the finer things in life. She had worked as a lottery seller but was displeased with her lot and enjoyed the company of wealthy men to treat herself. Her circle of friends and acquaintances was varied and broad, frequently being visited by many men and women. She was noted for her loving and hospitable nature as well as personally being both lively and funny. Police would later say that she had been a high-class escort, though many said she merely enjoyed a good party.

Sirkka-Liisa had spent the night of July 22, 1963, at a restaurant in her native Turku before returning home to Rauhankatuin around 1:30am, a street headed in the direction of the Aura River. She was in the company of a man who she'd danced with. It was the last anyone would hear from her.

At 4pm the following day, July 23, a friend, Saara Nieminen, went to Sirkka-Liisa's apartment to clean, an arrangement they had had for some time. She had her own key and became curious when she had to twist it several times to get inside. She quickly noticed there was unread mail on the doormat. She called out, asking if food was ready as was typical, and there was no response. Then she saw the blood.

Sirkka-Liisa Valjus was half-sat naked on the bedroom floor at the end of the bed; the flex from a boat-shaped lamp was around her neck. There was bruising to the head and neck, and she was very clearly dead. The room had been trashed during the struggle. 10 drops of blood between the bedroom and hallway were likely left by her assailant, this blood being what alerted Nieminen. Police confirmed that the killer had been injured himself.

They also recorded a violent struggle in the room, with a broken bottle near the body. There were fragments on Sirkka-Liisa's pillow, and the glass neck lay on the windowsill. A telephone table had been knocked over with the phone and an alarm clock having hit the ground. The victim's clothes lay in the middle of the room, and there was a small amount of money. This nor her other valuables had been stolen, discounting robbery as a motive.

It seemed that Sirkka-Liisa had been entertaining a man when he turned violent, with there being two empty glasses of red wine on the kitchen table. It may be safe to assume that it had been the same man with whom she left the restaurant. Inquiries into Sirkka-Liisa's background revealed that she had been attacked and beaten by a man around three or four weeks before her murder, leaving bruises on her face. She told friends that the culprit was a German sailor who became angry when she wouldn't let him into her apartment.

However, the mystery killer had been clever and tried to cover his tracks. There was ash in the ashtray, for example, but somebody had removed the cigarette butts. There was bloody water at the edges of the bathtub, and there was a 4x6 inch piece cut from the bedsheet, possibly to remove evidence. This is perhaps more likely to be the killer's blood rather than semen, as investigators recovered a condom at the scene. Maybe he used the material to temporarily bind a wound to his hand caused by Sirkka-Liisa using the bottle to defend herself.

Yet strangely, the attempt to scrub the evidence was only partially thorough, with the killer leaving both fingerprints and a palm print alongside blood stains outside the apartment itself. The most vital piece of evidence, however, was a bloody footprint found in the bathroom. The footprint was bare, giving a clear impression and suggesting the killer was at least partially nude, sex having taken place close to the time of the killing.

Interviewing witnesses, police recorded that the woman downstairs, Elma, had been woken in the night, sometime around 3am. She had heard sounds in the apartment above and believed it was furniture falling over. However, after the bump, the witness described the sound of a woman crying out "no." There was the sound of soft bangs, and then everything went quiet. The noise went on for about 10 minutes.

Another witness at the building, Matilda, reported that she had seen a man in the elevator who seemed "unwell." He placed his hand under his armpit as if to hide it from her and was looking behind him as he left. Her description put him between 27 and 30 years of age, 6 foot tall, and wearing a full dark suit with a white shirt.

A taxi driver, Einari, had taken Sirkka-Liisa and her companion from the restaurant to the apartment the night before. He described the man as speaking in a foreign accent and language, with Sirkka-Liisa struggling to communicate with Swedish. He believed him to be either German or Dutch. Witnesses at the restaurant said the same and that he had been foreign. They identified the language used as German and stated that he had told a German sailor that he was also a sailor.

Sirkka-Liisa Valjus. Public domain.

The suspect was described as being between 22 and 25 years old, between 5'10" and 6'1" tall, with light brown hair that was thick and long at the sides but cut short on the top. The suspect's attire was a source of disagreement between witnesses, with some saying he wore a dark brown suit while others described a gray-black small plaid jacket with dark pants. The wildly differing opinions suggest some confusion over the man or that perhaps Sirkka-Liisa had danced with more than one individual. His manner was said to be "childish."

Police initially believed the accounts from the restaurant in that the man had been a foreign sailor, possibly German or Dutch. There were 30 vessels docked in the harbor, and 17 of relevance were all marked for investigation. However, although dozens of sailors and captains were interrogated, only four ships had been investigated by the end of August. They checked footprints and appearance, and all those of interest were soon dismissed.

Where German suspects and Finland are concerned, one name will undoubtedly rear his head: Hans Assmann.

While much of what is written about Assmann is pure fantasy, the murder of Sirkka-Liisa Valjus is one crime he was actually questioned about in his lifetime. Assmann was known to be both violent and an alcoholic, and police were eager to speak to him for the killing.

At the time, Assmann lived in Sweden but had spent his summer vacation in Finland in mid-July, staying with a Finnish man who confirmed that Assmann and his wife had stayed with him until mid-July. Some witnesses alleged he had visited the deceased, being seen with her at local restaurants. Some also reported having seen the Opel car that he drove.

However, Assmann wasn't considered a serious suspect in the case. The night before the murder, Assmann watched television according to witnesses at his house, the suspect still being present the following day. Assmann's car remained stationary under his friend's window for almost the entirety of his stay, and the witness stated that the noise of the vehicle would have woken him if Assmann had gone anywhere in the night.

Speaking with the police, Assmann confirmed he had visited Turku, but only on three occasions, in 1954, 1955, and 1956. On the later occasions, he had been accompanied by a woman from Helsinki. He denied any involvement with the killing of Sirkka-Liisa Valjus, and after taking his footprints, he was dismissed from the inquiry.

Beyond Assmann, plenty of other suspects have been proposed in the case. One of the sailors, a Dutchman, was of particular note, having apparently just left on the ship Choklan. He was dismissed as early as July 27 when investigators announced he was not part of the crew. Another suspect was a sausage maker who allegedly had the keys to Sirkka-Liisa's apartment. He committed suicide two weeks later by jumping from his boat, his body subsequently found in the water.

Today, the case is long cold but kept alive by Sirkka-Liisa Valjus' son Hannu. Hannu was born in Helsinki but taken into care at just six months, being moved around to many places and families. When he was ten, he saw his mother's picture in the newspaper announcing her murder, with the effect on the young boy being almost unthinkable. Hannu urges investigators to continue looking into the case, and he has publicly stated that he wonders if Hans Assmann might even be his father. Sirkka-Liisa had always said that she would name her son after his father, and Hannau is the Finnish equivalent of Hans.

The killing of Sirkka-Liisa Valjus is the last prominent case linked to Hans Assmann and alongside the Lake Bodom killings, one that he was actually questioned about. However, police quickly dismissed him, just as they had done previously. With another solid alibi and his footprints eliminated, suggesting he is a strong suspect is difficult. The case then becomes yet another that remains long-cold, and it seems that police have little interest in investigating further.

It is an inescapable truth that the death of a prostitute or promiscuous woman never features high on the list of priorities for investigators, with many men having to be investigated and the likelihood that the killer might be long gone being high. Disapproval and the notion that the victim is asking for trouble prevail, yet nobody deserved the violent and brutal end of Sirkka-Liisa Valjus.

9 THE PERFECT MURDER OF MARIE LOCK-HANSEN

Denmark, 1967

The murder of Marie Lock-Hansen is the single most investigated killing in the annals of Danish crime. It was a murder that shocked a nation, yet remains a case that is little known outside Denmark, despite the immense effort by police and the public interest in the case. Over 50 years, 100,000 man-hours have been spent by authorities investigating the murder, and an astonishing 20,000 people have been questioned. Regular documentaries and books add to the intrigue, and everyone in Denmark seemingly has a theory.

While many unsolved crimes usually have a single prevailing view, the killing of Marie Lock-Hansen may genuinely be one of the most mysterious, with little indication of a real motive. The theories range from mistaken identity or a devious husband to criminal lawyers and even the KGB. Such is the continued interest in the affair that some have called it "the murder case that will not die."

Marie Lock-Hansen with her husband, Oscar Lock-Hansen.
Public domain.

Marie Lock-Hansen was seemingly living a good life. Born in Denmark in 1924, she had grown up in poverty, with two of her siblings dying early. She came from the working village of Lisbjerg, just north of Denmark's second city, Aarhus, where a farming community has existed since at least the Viking age. Marie was the first in her family to take the Higher Preparatory Examination that allowed her access to university.

She was eager to break away from poverty and rural life that stretched back generations. However, Marie's ambitions for herself didn't always tally with expectations of a woman in the 1940s. After marrying Leif Jørgensen in 1946, the couple were divorced in 1952. Two years prior, she had begun working at the engineering company Søren Jensen and Lock-Hansen in Aarhus. After her divorce, she married one of the owners, Oscar Lock-Hansen, in 1953. He was 10 years her senior, and the couple were unable to have children, Marie taking on her husband's adopted daughter. Alongside his work at the company, Oscar had taught engineering at Aarhus Technical College. He eventually sold his share in Søren Jensen and Lock-Hansen and devoted his time entirely to teaching.

The money received allowed the couple to move to an affluent address in Højbjerg, south Aarhus, and even employ a maid. Marie enjoyed the life that money allowed her, dressing well, with friends noting her eye for taste. She enjoyed antiques and trinkets, and the couple's villa was said to have immaculate decor. Marie had seemingly settled into the role of a housewife and didn't work full-time. She had initially set up her own business by the name of "ROLOCK" that provided duplication services for documents. It was based in Fiskergade, where Søren Jensen & Lock-Hansen had premises. She later moved the business to the basement of their house, and provided photocopying services to her friends and a handful of clients who primarily were her husband's colleagues. The enterprise had shrunk since having its own premises, with Marie no longer needing to work at the level she once had. By all accounts, it only survived as Marie wanted something to occupy her time.

November 10, 1967, seemed like a typical morning. Marie's business was unusually swamped that day, and she'd asked her friend and neighbor Lizzy Christensen to help, arriving a few minutes after her husband had left for work. The two set about their business, and at 10am, the maid, Irma Rasmussen, also came. Marie would usually help the maid in her chores for around 50 minutes before breaking for morning coffee around 10:50am. This morning was no different, and the two women carried out their usual routine, asking Lizzy to join them. Lizzy decided against the break and instead continued working in the basement. Just as they were about to start their coffee, the doorbell rang.

Marie opened the front door to a man and spoke with him. Irma Rasmussen, still sitting in the living room, couldn't hear the entirety of the conversation, but it seemed as if he wished to show Marie something. He was told that they were swamped with work, but if he was quick, he could enter. The man carried a folder. The two went across the hall to a small office and closed the door. Just seconds later, there was a scream, and three gunshots rang around the house. The man had secreted a gun inside the folder. Irma ran toward the commotion and came face-to-face with the assassin as he calmly tried to flee the scene. The killer told her to "be calm" and shot her when she became panicked. The bullet hit her in the right side of the groin and passed through the small intestine, bladder, and main nerve in the right leg.

Meanwhile, Lizzy Christensen called out in alarm in the basement, and Irma shouted that both she and Marie had been shot. Interestingly, the culprit could clearly have also murdered Irma, which suggests that Marie was deliberately targeted and with a specific purpose. The conversation at the door seems to have an air of familiarity.

Lizzy Christensen bounded up the stairs and quickly ran to a neighbor to raise the alarm. As she did so, she passed a man walking away from the house. His calm manner meant she gave him no heed. Irma Rasmussen, meanwhile, survived her ordeal and gave a description to the police. The gunman was between 35 and 40 and smartly attired in a dark cotton overcoat. He wore a hat, glasses and carried a briefcase. He could have quickly passed for a businessman if he had not just gunned down two women in cold blood.

Oscar Lock-Hansen was called out of his classes and returned home to the villa. The news of the tragedy wasn't broken until he reached the front door. Upon hearing the news, he fell to his knees and let out a scream of anguish. "They've killed her!" he cried.

The police began the most extensive manhunt ever seen in Denmark. With a who's who of Aarhus richest living in nearby villas, there was undoubtedly immense political pressure to gain a result. Witness statements from a butcher and driving instructor who were in the street suggested the man seen by Lizzy Christensen had entered a vehicle, a green Morris Mascot Mini Cooper. These statements indicated he exited onto Oddervej, one of the city's busiest roads that the house faced. Interestingly, soon afterward, the family of the driving instructor received a strange phone call from a man asking about the Højbjerg shooting. Only the police and family knew she was a witness.

An account from much later, however, suggests the man may never have entered a car at all, with a new witness claiming that a man carrying a folder and matching the killer's description, in fact, entered the nearby forest, which led to the Navy's Operational Command (SOK). Other accounts suggest the man actually got on a bus from Højbjerg headed toward the center of Aarhus.

The murder was a sensation, with the high-society couple and affluent location hinting a scandal. The seemingly "professional hit" style of the killing led to all manner of speculation, and the case quickly became a media circus. While many have openly criticized the police in the years since the killing, that might be unduly harsh. The likes of crime director Jørgen V. Iversen and crime commissioner Preben Nibe were dedicated to the problematic case and otherwise excellent officers. 40 detectives had been assigned to the affair, and they were most diligent. Forests were searched, and lakes dredged. But, the fact was, there was very little to go on, the police were inexperienced, and no proper procedures for dealing with such a case existed. The crime scene, for example, was never secure, meaning vital clues may have been lost. Key witnesses were not questioned to the depth that may have been required. With a description that could fit many men, the killer perhaps deliberately wished to blend in. The only real clue was the ballistics report, the car, and investigations into the background of Marie and Oscar Lock-Hansen.

The gun was a Walther P38, a German weapon that was the most common handgun in ownership at the time in Denmark. It had been the service pistol of the *Wehrmacht* at the outbreak of the Second World War and was in production throughout the conflict. Between 1945 and 1946, it was manufactured for the French military. Production ceased between 1946 and 1957 before it became the standard sidearm of the West German *Bundeswehr* between 1957 and 1963. While the gun offered no clues, being one of the WW2 issued weapons and from then Czechoslovakia, the ammunition used was of more interest. The gunman had used Geco 55, bullets that were primarily used by West German police. However, around 2,000 rounds had been imported into Denmark, with the majority being sold to the Danish military. The military issued Walther P38's to troops in Greenland, and troops being trained for those operations received instruction at the aforementioned Navy's Operational Command near the Lock-Hansen's villa.

Irma Rasmussen aided police in the creation of a

sketch of the suspect. The image was never released to the public as Irma was displeased with it, feeling it bore little resemblance to the man. However, the police privately distributed the artwork to police forces across the country, and the image became associated with the case. Irma was said to have near-photographic memory, and if she had rejected the picture, this was likely a mistake by the police. Indeed, Irma would be shown thousands of images of suspects over her lifetime and dismissed them all. Before she died in 2003 at the age of 87, police mistakenly showed her a photo of a man they had already run by her in 1968. Irma's memory was such that she could still recall the image being shown to her 35 years before.

In a case where every theory has been explored, Irma herself has come under suspicion in some circles. Police initially reported that she had stated in the ambulance that she opened the door, not Marie Lock-Hansen. The killer was seemingly unconcerned about Irma identifying him, despite having an open look at his uncovered face, and the shot taken toward her was apparently designed not to kill. In 1968, Irma demanded the police stop monitoring her.

The Lock-Hansen couple, too, came under suspicion. Indeed, while they presented a public image of total respectability, keeping up appearances to friends and colleagues, this was not the whole truth. Before the death of Marie Lock-Hansen, the marriage had allegedly already been troubled, and there was a rumour that Oscar had problems with alcohol. In 1965, 2 years before the murder, he had suspected his wife was having an affair. On November 3, just seven days before the murder, Oscar Lock-Hansen had signed legal papers that comprised a will and an agreement along the lines of a prenuptial. Marie had the right to everything should there be a divorce or Oscar died.

The police phantom drawing of the man who murdered Marie Lock-Hansen.

In his 2017 book, *Marie's Murderer*, Peer Kaae suggests that this document holds the key to the killing. Oscar already had a "son" by the name of Steen from a previous marriage to a woman named Vera. However, Oscar and Vera had adopted their daughter, Elisabeth (called Lisbeth), following the news that Oscar was infertile in 1947. Oscar began divorce proceedings when it became plain that Vera had had an affair with a political colleague and friend, Jørgen Peter Andersen. All parties wished to hush up events due to both Oscar and his wife's lover being involved in politics. Oscar agreed to lie and publicly acknowledge Steen as his child, paying a hefty amount of child maintenance in exchange for not being publicly shamed as a cuckold and infertile. Kaae suggests that this new document was designed to disinherit the son and that it was to be registered the afternoon of the killing. Jørgen Andersen, realizing that the form couldn't proceed with one of the signatories dead, came and killed Marie.

In 2018, a new book was published by Lene Pors, a young girl at the time of the killing. Pors is the adopted daughter of Jørgen Andersen. In the book, *In the shadow of Højbjerg*, she portrays a man she describes as "a psychopath," an immaculately dressed pillar of society and member of parliament on the outside while subjecting his family to extreme and sadistic violence in private. While she readily accepts the man was a monster, she remains unsure whether he was capable of murder.

"His behavior was extremely violent. He was a double man," Lene Pors told TV2.

While somewhat plausible, the theory doesn't fit the entirety of the facts. The document would have failed just as well if Oscar died, and there is no evidence that its existence was known outside the two signatories and lawyers. Equally, upon Oscar's death, the son would have inherited immediately had the document not been passed, making the husband a more likely target for assassination. Further, with Oscar having information that could have brought down the political career of Andersen, it seems a dangerous move to kill his wife. He was distinctly noted by police to have said "they've killed her" after being informed of Marie's death. Indeed, Oscar always seemed to know more than he was willing to share, drunkenly telling a friend seven years later that he knew who had killed his wife before vowing to never speak of it again.

The car, meanwhile, might very well be one of the keys to the affair. Sigvald Storm Mortensen, a lawyer, reported that his green Morris Mascot Mini had been stolen before the killing, making it an excellent candidate for the getaway vehicle. His law firm frequently used the car, and it was usually parked in a parking lot near his office in Frederiksgade. The car was soon found and examined, police concluding that it had nothing to do with the murder. Storm Mortensen was the lawyer for Oscar and Marie Lock-Hansen. The coincidence seems unlikely. However, his alibi was watertight, being in the USA at the time.

However, while Mortensen was in the United States, the affairs of the firm's clients were being dealt with by partner Hugo Schmidt. Schmidt has been linked with the killing in several works with the primary theory, again, centering on the agreement between Oscar and Marie. Despite the husband's attempts to portray married bliss to the press, it is said there was tension between the couple, and divorce was likely. Proponents of the theory contend that it is the divorce aspect that is key, not the will. Oscar wanted out of the agreement and told his lawyer so. The lawyer then killed the client. Stretching credibility, this theory fails to explain why Oscar would agree to such a thing in the first place, nor why one of Aarhus's best lawyers would murder one of his clients when he had no personal stake in the matter. That said, the man matched the description given by Irma Rasmussen and was 39 years old at the time of the murder. He had ready access to Mortensen's car and owned a Walther P38. The police are said to have tested the gun over a year later and found it wasn't the murder weapon.

The idea surrounding an illegitimate son and the insane rage of a former lover is not the only theory in the case, and Oscar himself came under suspicion. Some have suggested that he had his wife killed, enlisting Hugo Schmidt to do the job and gave himself an alibi by being at work. Others speculate that Marie had been swindling her rich husband all along. Some suggest she may have even blackmailed him into signing the legal documents at the center of many theories. With humble origins and as his former secretary, there was undoubtedly a strong smell of classism in the suggestions and no evidence that Marie married for money. Likewise, Oscar, despite his suspicious comments, seemed to deeply love his wife. Following her murder, he kept the house exactly as it had been during her life. He sank into many years of depression and turned to alcoholism, some saying he eventually died of a broken heart.

One theory was that Marie had been killed in a case of mistaken identity, with some suggesting she had been confused with Grethe Bartram. Bartram bore a passing resemblance to Marie and, during the Second World War, had become notorious for her treason and collaboration with the Nazis as part of the Gestapo, exposing 53 Danish resistance fighters for money, including her own brother, husband, and friends. She had been pardoned from a death sentence by King Christian X in 1956 and moved to Sweden, where she died in 2017 aged 92.

The infamous Walther P38 9×19mm Parabellum WWII German Wehrmacht pistol manufactured by Mauser AG. Bruce C. Cooper, Wikimedia Commons, GNU Free Documentation License.

Others suggest that a student angry at Oscar carried out the killing, the police pulling several young men in for questioning. Police investigated Oscar's one-time comments that Marie Lock-Hansen had a secret lover but again found no evidence to support the theory that she was engaged in an affair at the time of her death.

Yet, one more theory presented to police during the original investigation was that Marie had seen something she shouldn't. Located close to the Danish Navy's Operational Command, Marie often took her dog for walks nearby, and a few days before the killing, the pet had found a piece of discarded sausage left on her usual path. The animal eagerly ate the meat and became quickly sick. Taken to the vet, the dog was still there on the day of the murder, conveniently out of the house. When Oscar had allegedly confided in friends that he believed his wife was having an affair, he also told them he thought she had met a man on one of these trips out with the dog, traveling with the mystery man to Copenhagen. Friends are said to have confirmed this was true.

Some have speculated that Marie was carrying on an illicit liaison with somebody working at the base or even meeting for more nefarious reasons. These theories suggest Marie potentially worked for the SOK. A former employee has claimed Marie did indeed come around the base with an officer in 1961. He speculated that the officer was transferred to Greenland.

"I personally think it could be some spy who killed my wife," Oscar Lock-Hansen told the press at the time of the killing. "Not because she had anything to do with those circles, but because it was mistakenly thought that she knew something."

Writing in 2002, Eigil V. Knudsen revealed that a name and phone number had been written in Marie's journals, "Antik-Andersen." Knudsen states that this was a reference to her penchant for collecting antiques, and the man was an antique dealer named Kristian Andersen from Sønderborg. On February 17, 1967, Andersen had been murdered at his apartment in an alleged robbery gone wrong. Anderson was public with his money and enjoyed showing off, carrying wads of cash. He had a habit of flashing his well-stuffed wallet around at the local bar. The police passed this off as a coincidence, with Marie having bought antiques from the man before his death. Some have linked Andersen's name with Gustav Holm Haase, who was arrested in March 1968 and convicted of smuggling radio equipment that was to be utilized by East German agents in Denmark. There is, however, no evidence the men are linked.

Others, meanwhile, contend that Marie had been working for the opposition and publishing Soviet propaganda in her basement. In 2017, author Knud Simonsen published *The Mystery of Marie*, where he alleges that Schmitt was working with the USSR. While the book is described as a "documentary novel" and written as fiction, Simonsen insists that the basis is factual, and Schmitt ordered the killing, which was carried out by a Soviet hitman. The foundation, he claims, was that Schmitt was the man with whom Marie was having an affair and was involved in producing secret documents and letters through her basement business. Retired crime commissioner Preben Nibe described the theory as insane.

The journalist Poul Blak, author of *The Unlikely Killer*, meanwhile, says that he was told by Deputy Crime Commissioner Aage Haxell that the police knew the truth of the Højbjerg murder and that it "had something to do with either East Germany or the Eastern Bloc."

"[Deputy Crime Commissioner Aage Haxell] said he had confidential information. And by confidential, he meant that I must not let it be known that I knew of it, and for the same reason, I must, of course, not quote him on it either," Blak said in *PingvinNyt*. "Aage Haxell told me that in principle, the Højbjerg murder had been solved. I can not reproduce it verbatim here so many years after, but that was the meaning of what he said."

In October 2020, a new book was published by Christine Jønck based on the accounts of a source she names only as "Vibeke." Vibeke states that her now-deceased husband killed Marie Lock-Hansen in 1967, saying, "I do not just believe it, I know it was him."

"He was a salesman and had been in Jutland on the day of the murder. I could not understand why he did not come home because I was having dinner. The next day he went for breakfast, and while he was away, two civilian officers came and knocked at the door. They wanted to talk to my husband. They came inside, waited, and talked to him when he came back. They suddenly took him to the police station, and then I did not hear of it anymore. But it was strange because we also had a green Morris Mascot, just like the one that was wanted in connection with the murder."

Vibeke, without evidence, claims her husband had been a spy for East Germany and believes the picture created by Irma Rasmussen in 1967 is a good likeness. Interestingly, however, while it might seem that the police might have checked on everyone who owned a green Morris Mascot, this was not the case. They were more pointed in their approach, suggesting that the police may have had reasonable suspicion.

In October 2007, the historian Allan Vendeldorf wrote an article on the case titled *The Table Catches*. He states that the Lock-Hansen house had already been under surveillance before the killing, and intelligence services utilized a small green van outside their home. On March 21, 1968, the press confirmed that the Danish Security and Intelligence Service, the *Politiets Efterretningstjeneste* (PET), was investigating the case.

While the latest book may offer little new, it shows how much interest the murder still holds across Denmark, with the speculation around the affair continuing to grow. With few leads, everyone has a favored theory, be it espionage, revenge, greed, or infidelity. Preben Nibe, the former lead investigator on the case, doesn't believe any of them. The whole affair fills 187 feet on the shelves of East Jutland Police, and it seems that the case is no nearer being solved than the moment the killer walked out of the Lock-Hansen's front door.

There are points of note; the "stolen" green Morris Mascot is a huge coincidence. However, why would a lawyer be involved in a murder with nothing to gain? Nobody can say. While the KGB have reared their head, it seems that when there are no answers to be found, blaming the Soviets has always been the last resort of investigators with nothing else to go on. Many of these theories, which also appear in cases such as the Isdal Woman and Oslo Woman cases, amount to speculation based on Cold War fears rather than anything substantial. Equally, while there is no evidence, the guilt of Representative Jørgen Peter Andersen seems to be the theory that holds the most weight. That said, the phrase "no evidence" appears to occur repeatedly, and the case of Marie Lock-Hansen seems destined to forever remain unsolved.

It might just have been the "perfect" murder.

10 THE ENDURING MYSTERY OF THE ISDAL WOMAN

Norway, 1970

On November 23, 1970, a striking and cultured woman walked out of a Norwegian train station having deposited two suitcases. She would never be seen alive again. Six days later, her burnt remains were found at Ice Valley in the nearby mountains. Nobody knows who she was or what she was doing there. The discovery would trigger one of the world's most notable unsolved cases, and for half a century, the police and public have been intrigued at the death of the so-called Isdal Woman. There have been books, podcasts, documentaries, and pages of online forums dedicated to the case. While the specter of the KGB and Cold War fears of international spy rings loom large, other theories might hold more answers. She may even have committed suicide all along, just as the police claimed. Nobody quite knows for sure just who or what was behind the death, but modern technology is hard at work trying their best to finally close the file on Norway's biggest mystery…

On November 29, 1970, a man and his two daughters were enjoying a hike in the foothills of Ice Valley (Isdalen) at Ulriken, the highest of the seven mountains that surround the city of Bergen. The peaks are famed throughout Norway, and Bergen is often called "the city between the seven mountains." However, the area was notorious as a suicide spot, with origins dating back to the Middle Ages. Coupled with a recent series of hiking accidents in heavy fog, the area had gained the moniker of "Death Valley." It was on this cold morning that the nickname would become more apt than it had ever been.

Noting an unusual burning smell in the air, one of the man's daughters came across the burned remains of a woman amongst some rocks. The body was charred beyond recognition and had assumed the "boxer pose" that is often associated with burnings, the arms retreating back toward the chest. Fearful, the girl alerted her father, and the group quickly made their way back down the slopes to inform the police.

Bergen Police immediately began a significant investigation into the circumstances surrounding the unknown woman's death. Investigators cordoned off the scene and noted the woman's position, laying flat on her back, observing that there were no signs of a campfire that may have caused an accident. Around the body were a large number of items that some have said appeared to have been placed. However, this is likely not the case.

There was a pair of rubber boots at the victim's knees and the remains of a bag near her thigh area. Over a stone nearby was a woolen sweater, and on other rocks were the melted remains of two plastic bottles/ flasks, which contained water. The heat from the fire had also partially melted a plastic cup and spoon. With these objects out in the open, she may have been making a hot drink.

The police are met by this sight as they arrive on the scene on November 29, 1970. The Isdal woman is lying on her back between big rocks in the steep, wooded terrain. Bergen Police photo.

When the body was removed the next day, police found a steel ladies wristwatch marked "Solo," it had a black imitation leather strap. This watch was located near the left knee alongside a pair of earrings and a ring. Under the buttocks of the body was a fur hat that was said to smell of petroleum. There were also burnt remains of crackers or bread and some burned paper, which could have been anything. There was an umbrella, an empty bottle of St. Hallvard liqueur, a suspected plastic passport container, and the remains of a matchbox from Beate Uhse, Europe's first-ever sex shop. Peculiarly, the photos of the body from November 23 seem to show a ring on the left hand and perhaps an earring near the right ear, but this is less distinct.

The crime scene seems to indicate that the woman was having either a small break or picnic, with drinking paraphernalia paced out and the remains of bread or crackers found. Many tellings of the tale don't include this detail, leading to speculation that the body was dumped. Some involved with the case have not helped matters by describing the positioning of items in "ceremonial" terms when their location might be suggestive she'd simply stopped for crackers and a drink.

If the items were placed, it should be noted that it is known for suicide victims to often remove personal belongings before their death, particularly in cases such as drowning or immolation. Investigating the findings, police quickly realized that all labels had been removed from her clothing and the bottles found at the scene.

After leaving the body under guard overnight, forensic teams continued to work at the site the following day. Eventually, the body was taken to Gade's Institute for autopsy at Haukeland Hospital, with an autopsy being performed by pathologist

Johan Christopher Giertsen. The complete reports would come over the coming days, with the pathologist finding that the Isdal Woman had died from carbon monoxide inhalation. Soot found in the lungs indicated she had been alive when set alight. The woman had suffered a bruise to her neck from either a blow or a fall and had a small amount of alcohol in her system.

Forensic technicians search the site in Isdalen outside the centre of Bergen, on the day after the woman was found.
Bergen Police photo.

Alongside the alcohol were four milligrams of the sedative Fenemal which is native to Norway. Despite some belief, this is not a commonly used sleeping tablet. Fenemal is phenobarbital and is widely used to treat epilepsy and seizures. It is also occasionally used for sleeping sickness, anxiety, and drug withdrawal. The side effects associated with the drug are decreased levels of consciousness and a reduced effort to breathe. In the long term, there are concerns over dependency and an increased risk of suicide. Overdose can lead to pulmonary edema and acute renal failure through shock. It can result in death.

However, the dose in the Isdal Woman's bloodstream was not a lethal dosage, and the amount would be unlikely to have made her particularly drowsy. Instead, it would have produced a calming effect. An additional 50–70 tablets were undissolved in her stomach at the time of death, and therefore their effects played no part in her death. The jaw and teeth were removed from the body for tests, having have received unique gold-filling dental work at some point in her life. Working on the case in the modern era, professor Gisle Bang would later ascertain that this work had been done in Eastern, Southern, or Central Europe. Associate Professor Sigrid I. Kvaal preferred a more definitive answer of Eastern Europe.

The nature of the fire also threw up questions. Many myths also abound here, such as the presence of a large amount of petrol or the woman being on a campfire. This was never the case. Equally, claims that carbon monoxide poisoning in the open air is impossible are also false.

Despite some belief, her back was also burned.

"The body turned out to be quite burned in the back, while the seat/bum region seemed to be undamaged. We noticed that the woman's clothes were reasonably identifiable solely around the stomach and seat region," the forensics report read. "This probably indicates that she, during the first hectic part of the fire, must have been sitting bent forward and therefore somehow have shielded the said body parts."

The woman's fur hat found under the body was said to smell of petroleum, yet only a fraction of a drop was retrieved from the ground below the body.

The levels of carbon monoxide in the blood and soot particles in the airways suggested that the victim was alive. While she may have hit her head, the autopsy makes no mention of this. Police lawyer Carl Halvor Aas, one of the first on the scene, said it appeared as if she "had thrown herself back" from the flames. Police would later conclude that the Isdal Woman had been surrounded by a short-lived but intense fire.

"It was out of the way — it was an unusual place to walk. [There was] a strong smell of burnt flesh," Carl Halvor Aas, a police lawyer, would later tell the BBC. "The body was burned all over the front, [including] the face and most of her hair."

Ornulf Tofte, a former head of the Norwegian security services, the *Politiets overvåkningstjeneste* (POT), said he believed a small localized explosion might have been responsible. Speaking to the BBC for their *Death in Ice Valley* podcast series, he suggested that the woman was known to have a large can of hairspray, speculating that the canister exploded in her face, explaining why she appeared to have leaped back. However, any explosion would leave shrapnel and the remains of the canister. This would also apply to incendiary devices. There were no blast injuries reported to the body.

Original 1970 Bergen Police phantom sketch of the woman.

Investigators wouldn't have to wait long for a break in the affair. On December 2, a pair of suitcases were found in a storage box at the Bergen train station. The bags were deposited on November 23 and hadn't yet been picked up, despite the time paid running out. The police opened the suitcases and quickly linked them to the dead woman in Ice Valley. Inside the case was clothing, shoes, a wig, makeup, cosmetics, and eczema cream, all with the labels removed. Differing currency was found, Norwegian, Belgian, British, and

Swiss. Inside the lining of one of the cases was a 100 Deutsche Mark note, the former West German currency. There were maps, a timetable, and both sunglasses and regular glasses. On a notepad, the police discovered a "coded message" and a shopping bag for Oscar Rørtvedt's Footwear Store in the city of Stavanger. They would both be vital.

The items in the suitcases offer us some insight into the type of person the Isdal Woman was. From just a selection, a picture develops. While most markings had been taken off, there were Italian leather shoes in a plastic bag from Rome. There was a pair of Gant Neyret gloves in imitation snakeskin, made in Paris. Both these speak of style, money, and high taste. There was a nice trench coat with a possible fox fur collar and a fur hat in the Cossack style. In terms of toiletries, she possessed herbal shampoo and perfume by Jacques Esterel of Paris. It was a mixture of citrus and fruit, with a slight undertone of flowers. There was makeup from Paris alongside a wig in the "Napoleon" cut. One of the maps had the heights of Bergen's mountains noted on it. A sewing kit was from Hotel Regina in Geneva. There was a religious postcard and another that depicted a Norwegian winter scene of Santa Claus and his sleigh. There was a photo of the Madonna. She had a newspaper, *Dagbladet*, dated Saturday, November 21, 1970, and it is unknown if the contents held interest or it was merely the last one she had purchased. Police found another box of matches from the Beate Uhse sex shop, a link to the crime scene where the first box was found. There was a spoon from Vienna and a brown crystallized substance in a bag that looked like sugar.

Police later discovered it was indeed sugar.

Three of the great misconceptions with the case were also born here. The so-called "coded message" was not a cipher, nor does it really have any right to be called code; instead, it is merely shorthand with months and destinations reduced to initial letters. There were no "wigs" found in the suitcases, and there was only one in the Napoleon style. This haircut would be the one that is usually depicted in the police sketches. Equally, the police never found any of the supposed eight passports that the woman had used. The only evidence they had existed was that international guests were required to show this document at check-in, and, with differing aliases, it stood to reason that different passports were therefore used. However, the possibility exists that a successful con artist would have been able to circumvent this requirement. That said, to do this on eight separate occasions would be impressive. But the fact remains that the only possible indication of a passport was found at the burn site, and then only the one. What happened to any other documents remains unknown.

As police worked on cracking the "code," progress was made on tracking the deceased's movements. Making inquiries at Oscar Rørtvedt's shop, police in Stavanger discovered that a person fitting the description of the Isdal Woman had bought a pair of boots matching those at the crime scene. These boots were purchased in the city, and upon further investigation, police discovered she had checked into a local hotel under the name Fenella Lorck or Lorch. There was nobody by that name in either Norway or

Belgium, the country of origin she had given at the hotel. Just three days later, the notepad would be cracked, and the message was found to be a comprehensive itinerary for both Norway and broader Europe. The scale of the case and the potential for an international angle were now becoming apparent. It seems likely that the whispers of espionage had likely already begun. The investigation soon consumed the time of every member of the local police, and inquiries were made with Interpol.

Police sent inquiries to all districts, and a description of what the deceased looked like was issued, based on information from Rolf Rørtvedt, who served the woman at Oscar Rørtvedt's Footwear Store. The Isdal Woman was said to have been between 25 and 40 years of age, 5 foot 4 inches in height, with a small round face, brown eyes, and little ears. She had "long brownish-black hair" that she wore "in a ponytail tied with a blue and white print ribbon." The woman's fingerprints were sent to the Criminal Police Center in Oslo to check for a match, but police were left disappointed as nothing matched anything on record. Some claims have been made that the woman's fingerprints had been sanded away, but this is not the case, and a complete set was taken from the corpse.

The Norwegian press was now awash with speculation that the dead woman was a spy, and the headlines were certainly not without backing as the police suspected likewise. The security services, the *Politiets overvåkningstjeneste* or Police Surveillance Agency (POT) become quietly involved, a fact that the police would deny for decades. One aspect that the POT was particularly keen to investigate were reports that the woman had been seen watching a military test of new rocket technology in the west of the country.

Meanwhile, the code allowed police to track the Isdal woman to Trondheim, Oslo, Stavanger, and elsewhere. They checked forms at hotels across the locations and began to build a picture of her activities. Police discovered that she always claimed to be Belgian but used a wide variety of aliases, Genevieve Lancier at Hotel Viking (now know as Hotel Royal Christiania) in Oslo, for example, Claudia Tielt in Bergen. In Paris, she was Vera Schlosseneck. They discovered her movements via speedboat between Stavanger and Bergen. They found she had been in the country before, traveling out to Basel. Handwriting analysis conclusively linked the forms to the suitcase, and the fingerprints confirmed that the luggage did indeed belong to the Isdal Woman.

Witnesses were sought from the mystery woman's stay at the varying hotels across the country. Most told a similar story. The woman always claimed to be Belgian and spoke poor English, but she spoke French, Flemish, and German well. One eyewitness statement said they had seen her speaking in German with an unidentified man. She was golden-skinned and dark-haired. She often claimed to be a traveling saleswoman and antiquities dealer. She had an air of pride and sophistication; her style was noted. Her features, however, were less sure. Some said she looked Slavic. Others suggested she might have been from the Middle East. Others yet still thought "southern" or "oriental." At hotels, she was noted for knowing her wine, yet also for changing her room. One member of staff even observed that she had moved a table into a wardrobe to gain more floor space and that she seemed "afraid" to open the door. Many noted that she carried an odd "spicy" smell, with some saying it was garlic. However, this might be a mistake as others had pointed out that the smell was merely strong perfume, the staff at hotels saying that it hung in the air of her room even when she wasn't present. The fragrance, in her case, however, was fruity and floral.

Interestingly, the Mayo Clinic states that the apocrine glands in the body secrete an oily sweat when someone is suffering from anxiety or emotional stress. The fatty compounds produced are a breeding ground for sulfur-producing bacteria, making a smell very similar to garlic. The Isdal Woman is noted as being watchful and potentially paranoid, and the dose of tablets that had already been digested was said to be at a level that would produce a calming effect.

The "code," meanwhile, was found to utilize a straightforward system, and while it may appear to be a cipher at first glance, it is merely an abbreviation. For example, "24 M 31 M B" is "24 March — 31 March, Bergen". The details seem to be three sets of travel, one lasting from March 10, 1970, through April 3, 1970. The second period lasted from April 23, 1970, until July 18, 1970, and the final period lasted from October 2, 1970, until her death, the final entry marked as Bergen, November 18. No future dates were present, and the itinerary was all written with the same pen. The lack of other dates may be suggestive that the Isdal Woman never intended to leave Bergen.

The Isdal Woman's itinerary. Bergen Police photo.

Between March 20 and 24, 1970, she entered the country from Geneva, arriving in Oslo. She stayed at the Hotel Viking and used the name "Genevieve Lancier" before departing for Stavanger via aircraft. She then took the speedboat to Bergen and stayed at Hotel Bristol under the name "Claudia Tielt." The next day she moved to the Hotel Scandia and kept the same name. On April 1, she traveled from Bergen to Stavanger and on to Kristiansand, Hirtshals, Hamburg, and Basel. Interestingly, this trip seems to be unmentioned on the "code" with an "H" listed where the entry for April 1 would be, presumably Hamburg. On April 3, her itinerary listed her as being in "R" with no departure date.

Presuming the system remains consistent, in April, she travels to an unknown "F" and then onto "R" once more, followed by an unidentified "V" and a "W." In July, she is in "N" and again "R." Then she is at a "P," another "A" and then again "R." Some suggestions for these letters are Frankfurt, Venice/Vienna, Wolfsburg, Nuremberg/Nice, Paris, Amsterdam/Aarhus/Amiens. A bottle of perfume from Paris was found in her luggage, and, likely, the "code" was in French or German, which would mean non-English spellings (such as Wein) would change the outcome. "L" was almost certainly London.

Police accounts say that she was then out of Noway for six months, so all Norwegian cities can be discounted. The regularity of "R" is a point of interest and may suggest a home. It is the last listed destination listed in all three of the top columns. Where this is has never been ascertained, yet speculation suggests Rome, Rotterdam, or Reims. However, amongst the suitcase belongings of the mystery woman was a second shoe shopping bag beside the local one. This bag was from Nickol in Rome, a store that still exists today. Given the frequency of the "R," the positioning at the bottom of the columns, and the circumstantial evidence of the bag, Rome might well have been the base of whatever operation was underway. Also amongst the deceased's possession was a plastic Beate Uhse matchbox sold in Germany. While we know she was in Hamburg, this was some time prior; we could therefore speculate that one of the unknown letters in the middle column is in Germany, perhaps the "F." The matchbox was marked Flensburg, where the company had its first shop and offices, though all such boxes were marked this way.

Interesting points of note are that the woman changes the dating method between the first column and the rest of the document, initially placing the day first and then the month in the French, German and British fashion. She then swaps to the American style of putting the month first. This suggests the first column was written at a different time to the rest of the itinerary. Her October 3 trip from Stockholm to Oslo and on to Oppdal is not listed; the only known trip to not be on the paper. We can presume that "H" is Hamburg. However, her journey to Basel after April 1 is not listed, despite being a major city. This might suggest her trip to Basel was unexpected.

The final line of the "code" presumably is a footnote of something to be done on March 10 before beginning her first trip. It is not a flight reference, nor a car registration or British postcode that uses a similar style. If the line were a mixture of Latin and regular numbers, it would give us "105023 0 2000," yet this is unlikely, and the line should be taken in the context of the rest of the document as a simple abbreviation. However, ML 23 N MM contains an acronym we've already seen, "N," which stands for November throughout the rest of the paper. The first column of the "code" features the standard European dating system, and this line is in that column.

"November 23" is the day that the Isdal Woman dies. Being placed under the start date of her journey and with no entry beyond November 23, it could be speculated that this line refers to the end. That wouldn't necessarily mean a predetermined suicide as, having checked out of her hotel, it seems likely it was the last day of her trip in any case. If, however, the suicide theory is to be believed, given the slight religious overtones in the woman's life and her possible knowledge of antiques and art, "MM" might stand for "*Momento Mori*," "remember that you will die." The phrase is a reminder of mortality and is a type of classic Christian art. November remains the same in English and Latin, and taking it further, "ML" might well be "*Mane Lunae*," "Monday Morning." November 23, 1970, was a Monday.

Monday Morning, November 23, Remember You Will Die.

This last line seems to have been written simultaneously with everything else in the first column. If that's the case, then it's telling the Isdal Woman left no space for any further entries after November 23, also placing later trips in the middle column for symmetry. If anything further had been planned, putting the second set of dates (October 22 onward) into the first column would have been more likely. If November 23 has been preordained as a date of death, then suicide is apparent, and it's likely the date held some significance.

It's not impossible that the Isdal Woman planned an extensive trip around Europe as a personal farewell, having long marked out the date of her death. However, two postcards and names linked to saints do not make somebody devout. Equally, suicide is expressly forbidden by Catholic doctrine. "*Mane Lunae*" would also not be grammatically correct, all be it still making sense. However, we don't know if there was any level of proficiency or any knowledge at all. This theory, therefore, seems unlikely speculation, and the line remains a mystery, but it was likely something relating to a requirement before she began her journey.

In 2019, a new witness said he met the Isdal Woman in the French-German border town of Forbach in the summer of 1970, during this period where her movements are unknown. Wishing to remain anonymous, the man stated that he was 22 and believed she was around 26 or 27. They talked about painting and art, but she "didn't want to talk about her life and her work."

"I met a woman in a bar in the mining town in the summer of 1970. We saw each other for two, three weeks. She said she was passing through, a tourist, who was staying with friends... She was the one who told me where and at what time we would see each other..." the witness told *Le Republicain Lorrain*. "She had a Balkan accent... The woman whose name I, unfortunately, forgot spoke several languages. Her German was almost perfect, her French more academic."

The witness reported that he became troubled by strange phone calls the woman would receive, listening in with curiosity at what was going on. Investigating further, the man claims that he found evidence she may be a spy — the descriptions given tally with the Isdal Woman.

"They took place in a room. She knew the time of the

calls. She would put on music so that I wouldn't hear... I heard a man's voice speaking a language I didn't know. It sounded to me like it was always worried during calls. She said she had several papers and passports that allowed her to cross the Berlin Wall and go to East Germany without any problem. I rummaged through her things. She had two suitcases, not very large. There were wigs inside. She was also carrying two bags with very colorful clothes in them. Sometimes she would turn into an 18-year-old or a 20-year-old. She was very good at changing her appearance. It was amazing. It was during the Cold War. For a few weeks, I wanted to go to the authorities, the police, or the gendarmerie. I was afraid...."

The account is full of flavor and might be too good to be true, fitting almost perfectly with the well-known case while, of course, no name is mentioned. No passports were recovered from the Isdal Woman's belongings. It seems unlikely that many frauds would have been good enough to get across the highly secure Berlin Wall unless expertly produced. The account also doesn't tally with DNA analysis that makes the Isdal Woman much older. Intriguingly, however, the witness provided a photograph of the woman he says he knew, having stolen it from her as a memento. The resemblance is there.

The subsequent officially known movements came briefly on October 3 as the deceased traveled from Stockholm to Oslo and on to Oppdal.

At Oppdal, the Isdal Woman has an alleged encounter with the Italian photographer Giovanni Trimboli.

Trimboli owned his own company, GRAKO, and was known for his photos of Scandanavian landscapes and aircraft that adorned postcards.

He was born in Sicily on July 1, 1926, making him 44 in 1970. He entered the family tradition with his father and grandfather both being photographers. He worked on the set of Roberto Rossellini's *Stromboli* (1951) starring Ingrid Bergman and emigrated to the United States the year afterward. There he worked as an assistant cameraman and photographer in Hollywood during the 1950s. He became interested in landscape photography in America and published books in many countries, dividing his time between the US and Italy.

By all accounts, Trimboli was the stereotype of an international photographer, being a fan of both women and fast cars. Given the Isdal Woman's striking looks, it's no surprise Trimboli is said to have struck up a conversation. The playboy is said to have had affairs with women as far apart as his native Italy and the US, plus both Norway and Sweden. He is also said to have fathered many children. One of his postcards was found in the deceased woman's case, and after inquiries, he confirmed he had given it to her after inviting the woman to dinner.

While the Isdal Woman is usually described as unwilling to converse and all-business, here Trimboli claims he even took her for a trip in his car. She identified herself as South African and a saleswoman specializing in antiques. She is also said to have told him she had six months to see all the exciting places in Norway.

The trip to Oppdal is unique in the known history of the Isdal woman as it doesn't appear in her "coded" notebook. This may suggest that whatever the purpose of her trip was, it was personal.

Trimboli was seen in the presence of a woman on October 2 in Oslo. The woman was sitting in his car throughout a 2-hour business meeting, and the photographer told his business partner that he had just met her. Trimboli claimed this meeting had taken place at the office for Tourism in Norway and was giving her a lift. He told the same man that she was a wealthy Chinese student and headed for Stockholm. Later that evening, Trimboli phoned his partner, claiming to be in Oerje on his way there. However, that same evening he arrived in Oppdal, 284 miles away, and was alone. Here he told hotel staff that he had flown from Italy to Stockholm and come through Trondheim. The woman arrived from Oslo the day afterward.

The woman spent most of the day in the town square waiting for somebody and, after a day working, the photographer met her in what witnesses described as a planned meeting around 4pm. That evening the two dined with the hotel manager, and she claimed she was Chinese, living in South Africa. The woman said she would be going to Trondheim, and Trimboli said he was going to Oslo. She slept in the same room as the photographer, and neither went where they said they were going, ending up in Loen.

In 1971, the police carried out an extensive investigation into the whereabouts of Giovanni

Trimboli during 1970, discovering that descriptions of the woman he'd been with matched the Isdal Woman. During questioning, the photographer claimed to police that he met the woman by coincidence in Oppdal and that she hitchhiked with him to Oslo before departing in Stockholm. The next day, his story changes, and he claims he drove her directly to Sweden, saying that they took a trip to Helsinki and back after arriving there. The police acquired the name of the woman that Trimboli was with and checked with their South African counterparts. The woman was alive and seemingly not the Isdal Woman.

However, the woman in South Africa was no longer a student as Trimboli was saying, nor did she live near Johannesburg as he had claimed. The police seemingly never asked her if she'd been in Norway at the time. The alibi, however, falls apart when you consider the postcard.

The hotel manager had given the woman he met a postcard; it was one that Trimboli had given him some months earlier as part of a bundle. The manager didn't think it was available in shops at the time, which seems logical as it was a Christmas scene. The same postcard, with the same photographer and serial number, was one of the two found in the bag of the Isdal Woman.

On October 22, 1970, the Isdal Woman was in Paris at Hotel Altona, transferring to Hotel de Calais between October 23 and 29. On that day, she traveled to Stavanger and on to Bergen, arriving October 30, where she checked in at the Hotel Neptun under the name "Alexia Zerner-Merches."

At the Hotel, she placed a table in the small hall behind the door of her room. On another occasion, she was seen with a man in the dining room. Neither spoke, but she handed him a note. Upon reading it, the man is said to have become somber. Alvhild Rangnes, formerly of the Hotell Neptun, Bergen, observed the woman well and noted that she was sat beside two officers of the West German *Bundesmarine* (Federal Navy) on another occasion. However, Rangnes didn't record any interaction.

"Back then, single women in the dining room were not a common phenomenon. But this woman came in, with a proud posture, found a table, and settled down comfortably. She was obviously a woman used to traveling on her own. I remember I whispered to my colleague that I hoped I could adopt this woman's style as an adult," said Rangnes. "She made a lasting impression on me. She seemed so self-confident and aloof. But she was not really the type to don jogging pants and go hiking up in the Isdalen valley."

Between November 6 and 9, the deceased stayed in Trondheim at Hotel Bristol using the name "Vera Jarle" She then traveled to Oslo and on to Stavanger, rooming at Hotel St. Svitun with the alias "Fenella Lorch." She got a boat back to Bergen on November 18 and checked in at the Hotel Rosenkrantz, where she would stay just one night. A maid noted that when she had entered her room to do her sheets, she had inadvertently walked in on the woman. The maid found her in the company of a man. The Isdal Woman was sat on the bed, the man on a couch.

Neither spoke and the woman, dressed in black like every other description, was somber. The two seemed almost in mourning. She left the Rosenkrantz for the Hotel Hordaheimen the day after.

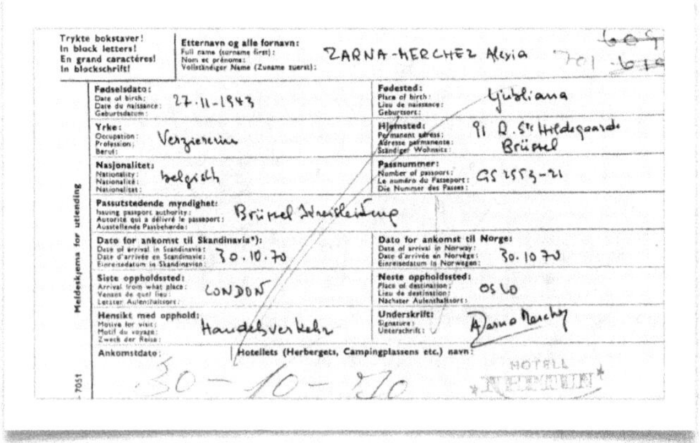

This is one of the registration forms the Isdal woman filled in. Both the name, address, and passport number turned out to be false. Bergen Police photo.

The Isdal Woman would stay at her new and final hotel between November 19 and November 23, confining herself primarily to her room and being said to be anxious and watchful. Staff at the hotel would say that she moved an armchair into the hall when she was in her room, adding weight to previous reports that she had also cleared space at earlier hotel rooms. There is also a report from Bergen itself which suggests she was in the company of a man at a furniture store. The two had argued before purchasing a wall mirror. This account is likely false, with the deceased known to have been in Stavanger at that time. It stands as a warning that all such statements must be treated with caution with mistaken identity frequent. Equally, "helpful" witnesses occasionally attempt to insert themselves into cases by telling police what they believe they want to hear, influenced by reports in the press. Reasons for this include vanity, mental illness, or personal vendettas.

Another witness came forward to say that they had seen her exchanging currency with a man on the morning of November 23. This was before she had checked out of her hotel, and the money was likely to settle her account. She got into a taxi and went to the railway station where she checked in the suitcases. In 1991, the taxi driver came forward to say that they were joined by another man before reaching the station. Some witnesses suggested they had seen smoke emanating from Ice Valley just around an hour and a half after this, though it can't be said that this was connected.

This witness statement for November 23 also poses a problem. While it is undoubtedly most likely correct, the woman confirmed by documentation to have checked out on that day, it contradicts a statement from November 22, which might suggest the woman was already dead.

On Sunday, November 22, a man was on a trip with his wife to the Svartediksvannet Lake in the Ice Valley. Both noticed a distinct funnel of smoke. The weather was said to be grey, with the smoke dissipating soon afterward. Given that the trip was on his day off work, the witness is unlikely to have made mistakes as to what day it happened. If this account is correct and the fire seen was the Isdal Woman, the only conclusion that can be drawn is that the corpse at Isdalen was not the same woman walking around Bergen.

Indeed, this would explain several discrepancies in the case. Witnesses never described the Isdal Woman as having a gap in her teeth, yet her surviving jawbone shows this is so. Future DNA testing puts the corpse's age at between 36 and 44, with eyewitnesses saying she looked as young as 25 and none suggesting a woman as old as 44. People described a woman with muscular thighs and wide hips, yet the photos from the crime scene don't tell this, even accounting for damage to the body. Equally, the DNA results offer no explanation for why witnesses believed she was of an exotic appearance, DNA information linking her to Germany.

In fact, the only thing that links the body to the suitcase is the fingerprints found on the sunglasses, which were also said to be broken. These could easily have been placed inside the bag. Notably, everything else inside had no fingerprints at all, even items such as the hairbrush. Suppose the woman on the mountain and the woman in Bergen are not the same, possibly as part of an attempt to fake a death. Maybe even a cover for a defection. In that case, the link between the corpse and the extensive itinerary around Europe and Norway is broken, meaning there are two mysteries to be solved. Equally, if the woman had been a spy, the body could have been swapped and repatriated in secret, all be it as a far-fetched idea.

To add weight to the theory that the timeline is

questionable, another eyewitness account from midnight on November 23 places the Isdal Woman as still alive and in the company of another woman and a man. Most believe the deceased had already perished hours before this point. Interestingly, the witness stated that the man and woman were seen at Isdalen in a large car.

However, all of that is conjecture and speculation. Almost all universally accept that the two people were one and the same. Indeed, there are plenty of witnesses who say the fire was on November 23.

Tore Osland, the son of Harald Osland, the lead investigator of the case in 1970, wrote an excellent book covering the issue in detail. The book, *The Isdal Woman: Death in Ice Valley* recants many of these witness statements about November 23 alongside the one from November 22.

A forest worker reported that he had seen smoke or fog on Monday 23, as did an army employee who definitively timed the smoke at around 12pm in the afternoon, believing it was a bonfire. A cyclist also saw the smoke and reported the same timing. Around 11:50am, ten minutes earlier, a firefighter unconnected to the reported smoke saw a man exiting Ice Valley. Assuming that the eyewitness reports of smoke on November 22 are false or a separate fire and the eyewitness report of the Isdal Woman alive at midnight on November 23 is incorrect, it seems likely the time of death was around midday on Monday 23.

Despite all the witness statements and the breakthrough in tracing the woman's movements with the notepad, the investigation would proceed little further. Despite obtaining the itinerary, nothing new would arise from subsequent studies.

The final reconstruction of her movements and aliases was as follows, and this is a direct quotation from the BBC's excellent article on the case:

- Genevieve Lancier, from Louvain, stayed in Viking Hotel, Oslo from 21–24 March 1970
- Claudia Tielt, from Brussels, stayed in Hotel Bristol, Bergen from 24–25 March
- Claudia Tielt, from Brussels, stayed in Hotel Skandia, Bergen, from March 25 to April 1
- Claudia Nielsen, from Ghent, stayed in KNA-Hotellet, Stavanger from 29 -30 October
- Alexia Zarne-Merchez, from Ljubljana, stayed in Neptun Hotel, Bergen, from October 30 to November 5
- Vera Jarle, from Antwerp, stayed in Hotel Bristol, Trondheim, from 6–8 November
- Fenella Lorch, stayed in St Svithun Hotel, Stavanger, from 9 to November 18
- Ms Leenhouwfr, stayed in Hotel Rosenkrantz, Bergen from 18–19 November
- Elisabeth Leenhouwfr, from Ostend, stayed in Hotel Hordaheimen, Bergen, from 19–23 November

Just before Christmas, 1970, Criminal Commissioner Oskar Hordnes met privately with officers at Bergen Police station, telling the team that the case would remain unsolved until the Isdal Woman was identified. On December 22, police held a press conference at the station and stated that suicide was the most probable cause of death, outright rejecting all theories that the Isdal woman had been a foreign spy. The case was shut down.

On February 5, 1971, the Isdal Woman was buried with Catholic rites at the Møllendal graveyard in Bergen. Police had made the connection to her possibly being a Catholic through the regular use of saints' names in her aliases. There was also the picture of the Madonna which had been found in her suitcase. The Catholic Church considers suicide a mortal sin. They will not conduct funeral services for persons who killed themselves, and they cannot be buried in a Catholic cemetery. While the official position of police in Bergen was that the woman's death was likely suicide, without an official designation, it seems that such rites were allowed. Her grave was unmarked, and the funeral was attended by 18 members of the Bergen PD. They ensured she was buried in a zinc coffin to prevent decomposition should she ever need to be disinterred.

Many of those working on the case outright rejected the official findings, with Carl Halvor Aas saying that "very few thought it was suicide" in the Bergen Police Department. Speaking to the BBC, Tore Osland noted that his father "could never put this case away" and was unwilling to "accept that they had to close down the case."

"Personally, I'm totally convinced that this was a murder. She had various identities, she operated with codes, she wore wigs, she traveled from town to town, and switched hotels after a few days. This is what the police call conspiratory behavior," said Knut Haavik, a crime reporter at *Verdens Gang* in 1970.

Since the death of the mystery woman at Isdalen, many different theories have been proposed surrounding what actually happened. Most favor the idea that the woman had indeed been a spy. Some suggest the hand of Mossad, who was at work in Norway during this period, four agents being arrested during the Lillehammer Affair of 1974. However, all those arrested during that incident denied any knowledge of the woman, and later DNA testing would suggest the deceased had no Jewish heritage.

The Isdal woman is buried in a zinc coffin which will not disintegrate. Bergen Police photo.

However, the Isdal Woman wasn't the first suspicious death in Norway, with several others being tentatively linked to the events in Ice Valley.

It was Christmas, 1962 when the body of a man was discovered slumped against a tree in Bardufoss. The man was quite dead. Police noted that there were no tracks around the body except the man's own and the skis of the soldier who had discovered him. Investigators initially suspected the man had frozen to death, his foreign appearance perhaps suggesting he was a tourist unused to the harsh Norwegian winter. However, the autopsy showed that the man had died from ingesting cyanide. The poison wasn't found in the flask of coffee he had with him or in his luggage.

The man left behind his belongings, and, unlike in most spy stories, there was a clear passport and visa being issued to Adnan Salim Maalou, born in Beirut, Lebanon, in 1933. He worked as a chemical engineer at a company in Lausanne, Switzerland. Maalou had arrived in Oslo the day before he flew into Bardufoss and told a flight attendant he was visiting a friend in Tromsø, telling staff at the terminal in Bardufoss the same story. Nobody came forward to say they had been the acquaintance.

Interestingly, the man had a map in his possession with a cross marked near where he died and in the pocket of his coat was a signal lantern with red and green lights. Why a man would fly into the Norwegian wilderness to signal to somebody and then take cyanide mystified the police. However, the airport and surrounding areas are some of Norway's most critical military regions and a base for jet fighters and helicopters.

The police were soon contacted by a doctor at Lovisenberg Hospital in Oslo. This doctor said that both he and a colleague had known the man during his studies in Switzerland. He added that he was hardworking and reliable, yet known as mentally unwell with symptoms we would today describe as bipolar disorder. He was buried in Tromsø, and some time afterward, his family in Lebanon paid for a tombstone that says simply, "tragedy or mystery?"

"We have reason to believe that he was somewhat unbalanced and that he had attempted suicide once before. The most obvious belief is that he has committed suicide under somewhat melodramatic circumstances," an anonymous detective was quoted by NRK as saying in 1967. "But we do not know. I am happy to admit that there are special circumstances associated with Maalouf's death."

On July 14, 1966, two children discovered a woman's body on the beach at Leka, an island north of Nord-Trøndelag. The deceased was lying facing the sea, half sitting and half laying against a boulder. All the labels had been removed from the woman's clothes. This was seemingly done at the scene of her death, and the remains of these labels were found in a fire close by. Also in the fire were her identification papers, photos, and a map. Discovering sleeping tablets next to the body, the police decided it was a suicide and didn't perform an autopsy.

Investigating further, however, the police discovered a trail of false names used in the Trøndelag and Helgeland area, using different British aliases and claiming to be from London. In Trondheim, she used her own passport and was revealed as 39-year-old Galina Bredemeijer from Amsterdam, then residing in Estonia. Speaking with her husband, a history of depression was seemingly revealed, the man stating that she had left home a month before. He never reported her missing.

On August 14, 1966, the body of a man was found in Borre without identity papers. Using a bill for a hotel in Iceland to trace the man's movements, he appeared to be Anders Karlsson of Jönköping in Sweden. However, fingerprints showed this was a false alias, and he was, in fact, Tommy Plath from Sävsjø in Sweden.

In cases that happened after the death of the Isdal Woman, it was on August 1, 1971, that a man was run over by a train in Nordlandsbanen, not far from outside Majavatn. The man had been decapitated, and there were no identity papers. Three years later, fingerprints discovered that the man was 27-year old Andriz Berzins from Würzburg, Germany. He had told his parents he was going on holiday to Belgium and France, making his presence in Norway a complete mystery.

Perhaps the most intriguing of all was the death of a Japanese man at Bodømarka. Discovered a short distance from the top of a mountain called Skautuva on September 19, 1976, the body had decomposed and clearly been there some time. A climber having suffered an accident or succumbed to exposure seemed likely. However, police soon discovered that all identifying marks on the man's clothes had been removed. There were no identity papers, and tickets from Stockholm found in his pocket had no name either. The mountain offered excellent views of several vital military installations, and speculation suggested that the man was a spy. These installations included a secret radio station for NATO's Atlantic Fleet and Defense Command Northern Norway in Skjelstad, north of Bodø.

The police put out worldwide alerts for the man, including dental records. They didn't have to wait long for a result, and just over a month later, police in Japan matched the descriptions to Tatsuo Hirata, a 24-year-old from Sapporo. In 1975, he had traveled to Hamburg to work in a Japanese restaurant. The job was only for a few weeks, and after it was concluded, he told his father back home that he wished to travel around Europe, doing odd jobs. His itinerary took him through Denmark to Sweden, where he was last confirmed to have been seen. Nobody knows where he had been in the interim or why he was up a mountain near secret NATO installations.

These cases may directly connect to the Isdal Woman, but more likely, they don't. However, they do show one of two things: either mysterious forces were at work in Norway, probably linked to espionage, or mental illness can often lead to people sadly committing suicide in the strangest of fashions. Equally, accidents can often seem suspicious through coincidence. However, in the case of the Isdal Woman, those coincidences may just happen too often.

While blaming the CIA or KGB is often the first port of call for some theorists in unsolved cases, the idea does hold weight when applied to the Isdal case. Somebody had to have financed her travel around Europe, and her apparent possession of multiple passports was suggestive of a well-powered organization. The removal of clothing tags, utilization of fake names, and a possible disguise are evocative enough, as is the witness statement that puts the woman in the vicinity of military rocket tests. Indeed, the witness is backed by documents that have been declassified by the Norwegian Armed Forces. These papers reveal that some of the Isdal Woman's movements correspond to top-secret trials of the then-new Penguin missile.

- On March 24, 1970, the missile boats were in Bergen. The Isdal woman was also in Bergen.
- In April, the team conducting the tests was in Stavanger. So was the Isdal Woman.
- On October 29, new tests were carried out in Stavanger. The Isdal woman was there.
- On November 9, there were further tests in Stavanger. Once again, the Isdal Woman traveled to the city.

The Penguin is an anti-ship missile developed in Norway with financial backing from the United States and West Germany. The rockets had been in production from the early 1960s, and US Navy test facilities had been made available for development. It was the first NATO anti-ship missile with infrared homing ability, undoubtedly making it of high interest to the USSR. The system would enter service in 1972, two years after the death of the Isdal Woman. It is still in use today.

Henry Kjell Johansen of the Norwegian Defense Research Establishment (FFI) was one of the leaders of the Penguin program and states that the entire operation was under close surveillance from the

USSR, with a high value being placed on the experimental technology that was under development.

A Penguin missile launches during one of the test firings in 1970. These test firings were top secret. Norwegian Armed Forces Research Institute photo.

"When we are going to shoot, a Soviet ship always shows up. Fishing boats or cargo ships often have an 'engine stop' just outside the shooting range," Johansen told NRK. "We receive notification of this from the Norwegian Navy, which guards the area. So it is clear that the Russians know exactly when we will start the test firing."

In 2016, the security services released the Isdal Woman's file to journalists, revealing new information about the case kept highly classified for 46 years. The files contained no indication that spy agencies had interfered in the investigation or shut down the affair. However, on the same day that the police held their press conference to declare suicide, December 22,

1970, the Armed Forces High Command security department sent them a message. By all rights, this message should have cast immense doubt on the findings about to be delivered to a waiting press.

"Woman found dead in Isdalen probably observed Tananger in November while tests with Penguin were carried out. The woman was also in Stavanger while similar tests were performed in April."

The newly released files also showed that the mystery woman's trip to Trondheim had coincided with two GRU agents in the city. The reports come from surveillance placed at Trondheim airport, working on a tip that two Soviets by the name of Rubanov and Popov were about to land. The tails reported that the duo was under watch at the airport, but they could not be sure that either man hadn't spoken with anyone during their time there. The two agents would depart for Sandnessjøen. It seems possible that these agents were Gennardi Fedorovich Popov and Aleksandr Nikolaevich Rubanov, two agents named by Viktor Suvorov in his 1982 book *Inside Soviet Military Intelligence*. Suvorov had served as a GRU officer inside the Soviet Union and at the United Nations Office in Geneva. He defected to the United Kingdom in 1978. Suvorov also briefly highlighted the work of GRU throughout Europe and named three names who had been working inside Norway for the Soviets. These were Valeriy Moiseevich Mesropov, Igor Ivanovich Zashchirinsky, and Lt-Colonel Zagrebnev.

Mesropov had served in the navy as an engineer with a Russian firm in Drammen between 1968 and 1970, attached to the Norwegian firm Koneisto Norge A/S. He was not a diplomat and was arrested on suspicion of espionage before being expelled on September 19, 1970, just two months before the death of the Isdal Woman. Lt. Col. Vladimir Zagrebnev, meanwhile, was the Soviet Embassy's assistant military attaché. He was reported to have visited a military area in the north and attempted to bribe officers and recruit agents for gathering military secrets. He was expelled in June of 1983. Most impressive, however, might be Zashchirinsky. Serving in Norway between 1974 and 1977, he was a representative at the Soviet Trade Delegation and engaged in clandestine operations to obtain information and products of a scientific or technical nature. This included material classified as top secret.

Others weren't named by Suvorov, including Third Secretary Yuriy Polyushkin and attaché Valeriy Yerofeyev, who were attached to the Soviet Embassy in Oslo. On April 11, 1973, they identified themselves as KGB operatives. They were expelled on espionage charges. Gennadiy Titov at the Oslo embassy was removed in 1977. A. Printsipalov, another third secretary, was discharged the same year. So was an unnamed chauffeur. Later, Aleksandr Dementev, Igor Izachtirinsky, and Yevgeniy A. Klimanov, all with the Soviet Embassy commercial section, were further expelled. Norway was a hotbed of espionage for the KGB. The theories surrounding the Isdal Woman enter this atmosphere of tension, all be it, with no actual evidence beyond coincidence and suggestion. It should certainly be remembered that in this atmosphere of Cold War fears, false accusations and suspicion were commonplace.

Interestingly, in 2005, Ketil Kversoy, a sea captain who lived in the area, came forward to say that he had seen the Isdal Woman a few days before her likely death while he was hiking at Fløyen, another of the mountains around Bergen. She was described as being dressed light, not equipped for the cold mountain air and rough terrain. The witness says that he saw two men following the woman, saying they were of a "southern" appearance, seemingly discounting Popov and Rubanov. By southern, it is presumed the witness was suggesting a darker skin tone associated with the Mediterranean or the Middle East. The Isdal Woman was said to look resigned and like she was about to speak to the witness.

"I was surprised. Some people were coming up the mountain. That wasn't normal. I'd seen nobody else, and I had been walking for a couple of hours… She was looking at me and her face; to me, it looked like she was scared and she was giving up… When she looked at me, I felt that she started to say something, but she didn't, and then she looked behind her and saw these men," Ketil Kversoy told the BBC. "I'm sure she knew they were going after her… I remember her hair, dark hair, not too long. And also, the men coming behind had dark hair. They didn't look Norwegian; I was thinking southern Europe."

Kversoy also said he was told to forget about it when he spoke to the police in 1970. Yet, this must be treated with caution. This account is often held up as evidence of murder and the involvement of espionage. It has a ring of being too convenient for helping the spy theory, just as with the tale of the woman being at Forbach. Retellings often omit that the witness had previously claimed to have been issued a gun when on holiday to Britain following his original revelation to the police. This impossible claim casts doubt on the veracity of the whole statement. British police have never at any time taken to issuing firearms to citizens.

"She could be a courier, I mean a messenger, because she traveled so much…a courier for someone else. Because, let's say you have a spy interested in the testing field for the Penguin missile: the spy would be living in that area, staying in that area, trying to gather as much as information as possible, establishing contacts with local people, with farmers or fishermen…" says Alexander Vassiliev, historian, and former KGB officer. "Now if she was somehow involved in espionage activities, she looks like she was a courier, passing information, let's say, from a person who lived in that area, to the headquarters of that espionage organization — to the handler."

In 2016, the case was reopened, and Norwegian media commissioned six new sketches of what the woman may have looked like from witness statements and photos of the remains. Journalists at NRK also made inquiries about the location of the woman's jaw removed for testing in 1970. After initially fearing it had been destroyed, forensic doctor Inge Morild found the remains in the archives of Haukeland University Hospital.

The Norwegian Criminal Investigation Service (Kripos) and the University of Bergen undertook isotope tests on the jaw and teeth, looking for chemical signatures that would tell them more about the Isdal Woman than could have been ascertained during the initial investigation. Meanwhile, the investigation team also recovered organ samples taken from the body and sent them off for analysis, seeking to obtain DNA.

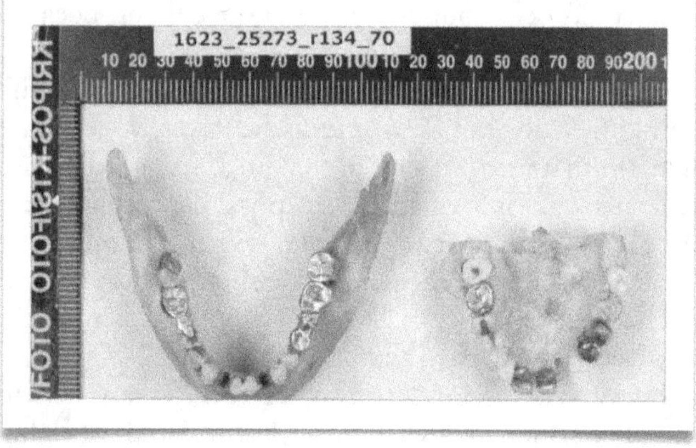

The Isdal woman had a number of gold bridges in her set of teeth, which is not typical of Norwegian dentistry. Kripos

The analysis results show that the Isdal Woman had been born around 1930 (+/- 4 years) and was European; investigators had always believed she was much younger, around the age of 30. The Isdal Woman herself gave her age as low as 28 on some of the forms she filled in at hotels, and the mistake means that some women known to be missing in 1970 may have been overlooked.

"She must have looked young for age, considering that she filled out the forms like this," Harald Skjønsfjell of Kripos told NRK. "It may also be the reason why she used wigs and other disguises — to look younger."

Phantom drawing of the Isdal Woman. Stephen Missal, Bergen Police image.

Further results revealed that the mystery woman had been born in Franconia, Germany, and almost certainly in Nuremberg. She moved to France or the French-German border as a child. This confirmed handwriting analysis from the 1970s, which suggested she'd had a French or Belgian education. Interestingly,

Forbach, mentioned in the recent 2019 witness account, would be within the region highlighted. However, the Forbach claim came after the public was made aware of the DNA results.

The dating of the woman's birth around 1930 in Germany brings the historical rise of Hitler and the Nazis into play. Between December of 1918 and June 1930, the Rhineland area between Germany, Belgium, and France was occupied following the Treaty of Versailles that ended the First World War. In 1936, the area was remilitarized by the Nazis when 3,000 German troops marched into the Rhineland and other regions along the Rhine, violating the treaty. The Germans began the construction of the Siegfried Line, featuring more than 18,000 bunkers, tunnels, and tank traps. Nuremberg, meanwhile, was a center of Nazism, with the city being seen as unique by Hitler and the regime, who noted its importance to the Holy Roman Empire. The famous rally of 1934 was held here, filmed by Leni Riefenstahl as a dark landmark of cinema, *Triumph of the Will*. It was home to the propaganda newspaper *Der Stürmer* and an important site for military production.

Whether the Isdal Woman's birth is closer to 1926 or 1934 is critical. If she were older, aged 7 in 1933 when Hitler was appointed chancellor, then her movements during that period as a child perhaps suggest her family fled the rise of the regime. However, had she been born as late as 1934, then it seems likely her family would have already fled if they feared persecution, and she would never have been born in Nuremberg. Her handwriting indicated French schooling and not German seems to suggest her parents were not Nazi loyalists who would likely have demanded a German education for their children.

While DNA results seem to exclude a Jewish genetic origin, as does her usage of Catholic saints' names, other parties such as gypsies and communists were also known to have fled the Nazis. If she had been born Jewish, she would almost certainly have been Ashkenazi which, though a history of segregation, would give a unique genetic variation that would have been quite clear.

If the Isdal Woman's family had remained in Germany and the heavily bombed Nuremberg, she would likely have been subject to being part of the *Erweiterte Kinderlandverschickung* program (KLV). This program was designed by the Nazis to evacuate children from the big cities, such as Nuremberg. The intent was to provide the children with nutrition and safety while these places remained under allied attack. The program was equally designed to indoctrinate the children into the *Volksgemeinschaft*, or "people's community," and there is no way a French education would apply. Therefore it seems safe to suggest that the Isdal Woman's family had left Germany before the war, and this is unlikely to have been into German-occupied Rhineland and likely to be to the French-speaking Walloon region of Belgium or into northern France near the border.

With the woman being born in Nuremberg and being educated somewhere around the intersection of France, Germany, and Belgium, it seems unlikely that the Isdal Woman was working for East Germany.

However, if that was the case, it might explain why nothing was ever found in terms of records, with the Stasi destroying a great many files following the regime's fall in 1989, at first using shredders and then by hand.

The Isdal Woman consistently gave her nationality as Belgian. While this might be a lie like so much more, it's unlikely that somebody wishing to hide their identity would expose themselves to being caught out by being unable to converse about their home country. The Walloon Region has a small German-speaking community that comprises around 1% of the population located in the east. This area is known as the Eupen-Malmédy and consists of three administrative cantons around the small cities of Eupen, Malmedy, and Sankt Vith. The region had initially been German and lost at Versailles, being reannexed in 1940.

The Catholicism of the Isdal Woman is often in the background. Not only was there the photo of the Madonna and postcard, but saints names were used, such as Genevieve and Vera. Also, the street names she gave as addresses were linked to religion. Rue Sainte-Walburge 18, Place Sainte-Walburge 17 (Stated as being in Brussels), 2 Rue Sainte-Walburge (Stated as being in Leuven), and Rue de la Madeleine 3 (Stated as being in Brussels). All of these addresses are in Liège, despite her identifying them as elsewhere. There is also a very famous Rue de la Madeleine in Paris.

Another address used, "Philipstockstr," seemingly references Philipstockstraat, located in Brugge, not

Brussels. It is close to many museums and the Basilica of the Holy Blood. This basilica houses a holy relic that is purported to be the blood of Jesus, collected by Joseph of Arimathea. Both Trondheim and Oslo have Catholic cathedrals, two of only three in the country, and the likelihood that she visited Rome more than any other city has been explored. If the Isdal Woman was a Catholic and was from a devout family or community, she may have killed herself far away from home to spare them spiritual anguish. At Place Sainte-Walburge is the Church of Saint Walpurga.

Meanwhile, given in Oslo, Rue Sainte-Hildegarde doesn't exist at all and perhaps shows that she had never been to the locations in Liège, simply inventing place names. There is a reference to Rue Sainte-Hildegarde in Marcel Proust's immense seven-volume *In Search of Lost Time*. Coincidentally, the work features the "episode of the Madeleine," which occurs early in the first volume, *Swann's Way*. This is the same volume that features Rue Sainte-Hildegarde. Witnesses to the Isdal Woman noted that she was seen reading books and keeping mostly to herself. None of these books were recovered, but it's certainly possible she read Proust. The book accounts childhood and early adulthood experiences in late 19th century and early 20th century aristocratic France. One theme of the work is involuntary memory, with the narrator's memories being triggered by sensory experiences such as sights, sounds, and smells. However, it's more likely that the Isdal Woman simply failed to coincidentally create a real place name on this occasion, inventing the street based on Saint Hildegard of Bingen.

Saint's Names Used in Addresses.

Saint Hildegard of Bingen is an interesting choice. Until her equivalent canonization by Pope Benedict XVI in 2012, she wasn't considered a saint by the entire Catholic Church, even though she had been venerated for centuries in practice. She is regarded as one of the founders of scientific natural history in Germany, and her shrine and relics are at Eibingen Abbey in Hesse, Germany. Her feast day is September 17. Saint Hildegard is of particular interest to feminists and the New Age movement, having spoken on holistic and natural healing alongside her status as a mystic. She advocated many foods, including garlic and porridge, which the Isdal Woman regularly had for breakfast. Hildegard was also believed to have been epileptic, the actual cause of her famous visions.

The French Saint Madeline was the founder of the Society of the Sacred Heart, her shrine being at St Francis Xavier's Church in Paris. More than 100 schools were opened by the Society of the Sacred Heart worldwide, and she is the Paton Saint of schoolgirls. There were such schools in places of note, including Brussels, Hamburg, Rome, and London.

Saint Walpurga was born in England but died at Heidenheim, in Germany. She is the Patron Saint of Antwerp and both Eichstätt and Weilburg in Germany. She is particularly notable in Northern Europe and Scandanavia through Walpurgis Night which is celebrated on the night of April 30 and the day of May 1, her feast day. Walpurga was lauded by

Christians in Germany for battling "pests, rabies, and whooping cough, as well as against witchcraft." The day is marked by bonfires and other activities to ward off witchcraft. There is a St. Walburga Church in Antwerp.

Saint's Names Used as Aliases

Saint Genevieve is the patron saint of Paris. Her feast is on January 3. Her attribute is a candle, and it is said the Devil blew it out when she went to pray at night. A candle stump was amongst the items in the Isdal Woman's suitcase. In the era of electricity, it seems possible this would have been for religious purposes.

The Isdal Woman used the name Claudia twice, and there are also several Saint Claudias. There are two martyrs by the name, but it is more likely this refers to the first-century saint of who little is known. The history of this figure is debated, but the popular theory is she was the British mother of Linus, the second Pope. A second view names her as Claudia Rufina, a 1st-century British woman living in Rome. Her feast day is August 7.

Saint Vera of Clermont was French, and little is known of her. Her relics are enshrined in the church of Saint Artemius in Clermont, France.

There are innumerable Saint Elizabeths such as the German Elisabeth of Schönau, Elizabeth, the mother of John the Baptist, and Elizabeth of Aragon. However, this is probably a reference to Elizabeth of Hungary, the patron of the Third Order of St. Francis. She died in Hesse, Germany, and is significantly associated with Franciscans. Her day is November 19, and there is a shrine in her honor at St. Elizabeth's Church in Marburg, Germany. Elizabeth has many other patronages, including hospitals, nurses, exiles, homeless people, and widows.

From this list, we can see that all the saints used were female, with none being male. While understandable in the names she was choosing as her aliases, this continued in the words she chose as street addresses. Equally, there is a strong Germanic influence here alongside the French.

The bottle of Kloster liqueur is also interesting. This alcohol is brewed by monks at Ettal Abbey in Bavaria. It is not the kind of drink you might have expected to associate with somebody frequenting the fashion districts of Paris and Rome. Ettal is a Benedictine monastery, and there are Benedictine themes through many of the listed saints. There is also a notable marble statue of the Madonna and Child at the abbey. It would be interesting to know where the Isdal Woman's photo of the Madonna was taken. Was it a personal photo or a souvenir from a gift shop, perhaps?

Another contender for the photo is possibly the most famous Madonna and Child, Michelangelo's statue at the Church of Our Lady in Bruges. Interestingly, also in Bruges, you'll find the Princely Beguinage Ten Wijngaerde, a convent for Benedictine nuns. It had once been a beguinage but in 1929 was turned into a regular nunnery by the then Mother Superior Geneviève de Limon Triest. Geneviève was a name used by our mystery woman. At the entrance, Saint

Elizabeth of Hungary can be seen. Elizabeth was again one of the names used by the deceased. De Wijngaard is also devoted to Saint Alexius. The woman used Alexis as a name. Instead of the fictional street of Rue Sainte-Hildegarde, had the Isdal woman meant "Wijngarde"? At 44 years of age, the Isdal Woman had never given birth, unusual for the era. Could she have spent time in a convent? Or could her claims of working in antiques mean a background or expertise in theology or religious history/buildings? Perhaps she was educated in a convent school.

Police certainly believed beyond doubt that she was a Catholic through this repetitive use of religious saints, also noting the religious postcards in her suitcase and probably the candle. Her liking for fashion and style certainly doesn't stand against her being religious. However, two images and some names she may have been familiar with from her family or wherever her home might be certainly doesn't stand as evidence of deep-seated beliefs. The deceased wore no crucifix, had no bible, and showed few other signs of religious devotion, with no known trips to places of worship.

Indeed, the information presented by the Isdal Woman on the hotel forms is intriguing and poses a significant problem for the prevailing theory of espionage. She gave varying professions such as *Antiquitätenhändlerin* and *Verziererin*, an antique dealer and a decorator or ornamenter, the word applying to a specialist to adorns pottery. She told the receptionist at St. Svithun Hotel in Stavanger that she was an interior decorator. It seems likely that she would have had a working knowledge of these professions for such conversations. However, the forms are also full of simple mistakes that were instantly recognizable to the trained eyes of the police. These are mistakes that would not have been made by a GRU agent. Equally, an agent would never have utilized differing passports and identities, making it evident what they were. Agents instead would have a single false identity that was as watertight as it could possibly be, making few mistakes that might prove they weren't who they said they were.

In fact, when you remove the hyperbole about the "code" on the notepad being a cipher and see that all the Norwegian security services could find on the woman was that she had been in a few coincidental places, the spy theory begins to collapse. This is only amplified when coupled with her unprofessional behavior. Even the wig may have a simple enough explanation. With the scalp burned away, the possibility exists that the deceased simply suffered from alopecia, and we don't know. The woman had eczema cream in her suitcase, and it is not unusual for sufferers of atopic dermatitis and other forms of eczema to also suffer from alopecia areata. Equally, she may have simply wished to wear a wig as a fashion statement.

If not a trained intelligence agent, then the question of criminality might come into play, with organized crime groups often utilizing covert methods that can seem similar. These methods, of course, not being as thorough or successful as professional spies. The itinerary of the Isdal Woman might be suggestive that she worked as a courier and her manner said to be morose and paranoid may even suggest she was working against her will.

Whether a spy, criminal, or otherwise, the possibility exists that the Isdal Woman was not murdered for her part in whatever was happening. She may, indeed, have committed suicide. Her location on the mountain stands as direct evidence. It is unlikely anyone would have gone to the trouble of forcing someone toward such an inaccessible spot where they may have been openly seen, or the victim had the potential to even make a getaway. Had the killing been an assassination, there would have been dozens of lower-lying spots, locations in Bergen, or even right in her own hotel. Also, while state-murder can often be carried out by poisoning, this would be through food or drink poisoned with a deadly substance such as arsenic or cyanide, not a sedative.

Indeed, the presence of Fenemal is also suggestive. Reports that the Isdal Woman seemed on edge from many witnesses has been taken as evidence she was followed, yet it's also possible this was anxiety. Fenemal is sometimes used to treat anxiety and has a calming effect. It is possible that the woman took the entire bottle believing the dose would be fatal. However, perhaps not.

The drug is also used to treat epilepsy and seizures. Had the woman been suffering from attacks, it may explain why she stayed in her room and ensured the floor space was clear. It would also explain the significant bruise to her neck. Depressed by her condition, she may have committed suicide. There has been a considerable stigma attached to those with epilepsy. For example, in the United Kingdom, it was considered grounds for the annulment of marriage until as late as 1971. The risk of suicide is between two and six times higher in those with the condition.

Some people can become aware of a warning "aura," such a taste or smell that allows them to know that a seizure is imminent. If this aura is a smell, some people can fight off the attacks by sniffing a strong odor such as roses or garlic. This aura allows the sufferer to sit or lay down, so they don't fall. Suppose the Isdal Woman had become aware she was about to have a seizure on a dangerous mountain. In that case, it's possible she panicked and took the entire bottle of Fenemal, believing this would help, having no intention of suicide. Accidents involving those suffering from seizures are common and, had the woman been trying to start a fire when she had the attack, it wouldn't be beyond possibility that it was an accident. The crime scene shows that bread or crackers were present, and cups had been placed on rocks containing water. A conclusion that the woman had stopped for a break or a small picnic and was looking to heat something up is not unreasonable.

The eczema cream found in the Isdal Woman's bag contained paraffin, and reports from 2018 highlighted the fact that creams to treat dry and itchy skin can build up over time in fabrics and cause them to catch fire more easily. Fifty such deaths have been reported by UK fire and rescue services.

"It was previously thought the risk occurred with emollients that contained more than 50% paraffins. But evidence now points to a risk with all emollients, including paraffin-free ones." The BBC once reported.

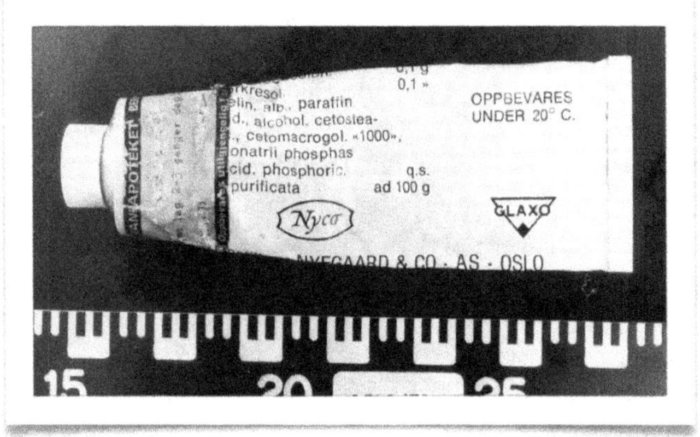

The cream found in the woman's suitcase. Bergen Police photo.

Patients were warned not to go near naked flames. If the eczema of the Isdal Woman were on her front, the paraffin would have collected in her clothes only in those areas, not so much on her back. This would explain the lack of gasoline found in any of the bottles. If, as speculated, she was using this cream on her head, hence the wig, it would explain why the fur hat allegedly smelled of gasoline. The smell was, in fact, the eczema cream. The forensics report stated: "Smell indicated that it contained remains of petroleum or something similar."

A picture then develops of a woman more rounded than the femme fatale of the spy theories. A dignified and beautiful woman, yet suffering from seizures, eczema, and alopecia, perhaps anxiety too. She removes furniture as she fears banging her head on it in her hotel room. She hurts her neck during one such seizure and carries garlic to help avert them. Perhaps she seeks religious solace; maybe she thinks Lake Geneva or the Bergen mountain air may help her. Hotel Regina is only eight minutes away from Lake Geneva, after all. Calm relaxing places. Men approach her, of course. Such is life as a single woman traveling through hotels. One gives her matches, perhaps when he lights her cigarette. Maybe she is divorced or widowed, having the money to explore. She has fun at times, the photographer and his fast car. Yet, she is also often depressed and doesn't want to talk. This is a journey for herself.

Having already marked the heights of the mountains, she decided to take the air at Ulriken. She takes some Fenemal and sets out on her journey. The woman stops for a rest at Isdalen and, to go with crackers, she decides to take a drink. She places her tartan shawl on the ground like a blanket. She was known to smoke, and none were found in her suitcase; it seems likely they had been in her pocket and incinerated with her clothing. Lighting a cigarette on a break would be a normal thing to do. However, the woman knows a seizure is coming and takes a lot more Fenemal in a panic, worried about the dangerous terrain. She sits down as she knows how to do, and feeling better or seeking a calming effect, she lights a cigarette. The seizure happens as she's puffing away, and she drops the lit cigarette into her coat. It smolders in her clothing and soon finds the paraffin of the eczema cream. Seconds later, her clothes burst into flame with just enough paraffin to fuel a short and intense fire. The fire or the seizure sends her backward, hitting her head on the rock. This she would likely have survived.

In February 1991, two hikers in Oregan discovered the burning body of a murdered woman. The deceased had been stabbed and set on fire. The flames consumed the soft tissue of the body. Meanwhile, the area between the mid-chest and knees was destroyed, and forensics teams did not recover the pelvis and spine. If you examine the crime scene photos from Isdalen, you will note the majority of the worst damage to the Isdal Woman is the same region between the chest and knees. The combined conditions of a well-oxygenated outdoor environment, accelerant and an immobile clothed body created what is known as "the wick effect." This is where the human body's fat melts into the clothing, continuing to fuel the fire. This effect would mean that little accelerant was needed, and the body itself fed the flames. Indeed, at the bottom of the scree, Bergen police found large amounts of a yellowish, fat-like material alongside heavily blackened stones, which shows the fire was present here at the bottom. The dripping fat was initially aflame.

The infamous 1951 Mary Reeser "spontaneous human combustion" case was, in reality, caused by the wick effect. Forensics teams found melted fat and that nearby plastic objects had melted and lost their shape. In 2006, a man in Geneva was near incinerated from a single cigarette that he dropped on himself after a heart attack. The flammability of the cream is probably not even an issue. If the woman had suffered a seizure and hit her head, then a lit cigarette and the wick effect would have been enough to kill an unconscious woman. In short, no gasoline was ever needed to burn the Isdal Woman.

Indeed, the forensics team believed that the body had been on fire twice. This would be the initial fire from the cigarette and then the fire fuelled by the body. They reported that there was "extensive damage at the knees of the body, calves and lower thighs suggests, however, that a subsequent fire of a more prolonged nature has arisen here."

While that theory may sound good, it fails to explain why labels were removed from her clothes, shoes, and bottles and why she lied about who she was. Equally, is it likely that somebody intelligent would have panicked and taken so many pills? Like all ideas, it doesn't tie all the ends together. While this theory tells the end of the Isdal Woman's story, it fails to reveal the beginning.

If, however, the line on the Isdal Woman's code did mean "Monday Morning, November 23, Remember You Will Die" (*Mane Lunae* November 23 *Momento Mori*), then the death of the Isdal Woman can not have been anything but suicide. The tale becomes one of great sadness, of a woman who planned her death nine months before events at Isdalen. Her travels around Europe are perhaps a farewell tour of sorts, blazing through the money she knows she'll never need. The use of Latin would add some weight to an idea she had once been a part of religious orders, never having children and devoting herself to God. Perhaps she lost her faith, hence no crucifix or Bible, wishing to experience life before death with fashion and Italian photographers. Maybe anxiety or epilepsy caused issues; the church once described it as "holy madness" after all. With her family and friends perhaps knowing of her troubles, they would undoubtedly worry. Once she vanished, she needed to ensure they'd never find her and stop her plans, maybe also wishing to save them the shame associated with suicide in Catholicism. So she had to become "Fenella Lorch," "Claudia Tielt," and all the others. On Monday morning, November 23, she climbs into Ice Valley and takes her tablets as planned. Whether she starts the fire herself or it happens accidentally, the predetermined result is the same.

Some have speculated that the Isdal Woman may have been a terrorist, possibly from a left-wing group such as the Red Army Faction (RAF), aka the Baader-Meinhof Group. The RAF was formed in West Germany in 1970. There is little evidence for this. The crime writer Gunnar Staalesen has said that his personal theory "is that she was hunting for Nazi war criminals… Israel and Norway had a very friendly connection, so if the secret services knew that was what she was doing here, they would keep that a secret. But it's only a theory."

Others suggest she may have been a high-class escort, traveling to meet wealthy clients across Europe. The evidence for this is that the matchbox found by the body was only sold through sex shops. In his book *The Woman in Isdalen Valley*, the author Dennis Zacher Aske suggests that the woman was killed by an individual he names as "an Italian photographer," and they had been traveling together for some time. Many of the sightings of the Isdal Woman with a man had been the photographer. Therefore, her sullen behavior may have been the result of an abusive relationship, this "Italian photographer" apparently having been previously charged with rape, threatening behavior, and acts of violence. What was a simple case of a domestic killing became sensationalized by the tabloid press, pushing the security services to investigate something that was essentially nothing more than coincidence. Indeed, if one of the woman's clients had been in the Norwegian military, her movements may have coincided with some of the Penguin missile tests. Her involvement in prostitution meant that it was unlikely anyone would be willing to come forward and admit to being a client. Perhaps, wanting a way out, she decided to end her life or make a grand statement that went wrong. The man argued with her, resulting in a blow to the neck. Perhaps he forced her to take the tablets. Whether by design or accident, she was set on fire.

However, while the ideas are certainly plausible, it fails to account for the level of secrecy involved. While prostitution was undoubtedly illegal, would the Isdal Woman really have needed to cut the labels from her clothes? The police dismissed the theory that the Isdal Woman was a prostitute in 1970. All the hotels in which she stayed were strict in their policies regarding prostitution, and she could easily have stayed elsewhere. She never brought anyone into the hotels and was noted for being alone most of the time. Equally, the use of holy names and religious images, including the Madonna, suggest she was a practicing Catholic. If the theory is rejected, the question as to where she got the Beate Uhse matchbox remains.

The suggestion that the matchbox indicates prostitution comes perhaps from a misunderstanding of Beate Uhse shops. While the image of a sex shop is of a seedy and boarded-up hovel with a pervert behind the counter, Beate Uhse is a chain more comparable to Britain's Ann Summers. They are well lit and inviting, selling lingerie alongside the likes of sex toys. The matchbox, equally, could have been obtained as a corporate gift from a trade fair or an event sponsored by the company. During the late 1960s and 1970s, Beate Uhse was trying to change the image of the sex shop and make the business mainstream. For example, on September 6, 1970, they sponsored the Love and Peace Festival on the German isle of Fehmarn. This open-air event would be the last festival appearance of Jimi Hendrix before his death.

Another interesting theory came from former Chief of the Bergen Police, Asbjørn Bryhn, who suggested in 1976 that the Isdal Woman had been involved in a check fraud scheme. The press were derisory in response, wanting tales of spies and femme fatales. Yet, the idea is certainly not as absurd as they made out.

This scheme involved money being paid into bank accounts in Malmö, Sweden. Checks associated with the account were then copied and cashed at banks in the Netherlands and Norway. They used fake passports while doing this and traveled extensively. An individual by the name of "Fellin" received the stolen money and escaped Sweden.

In 1972, four arrests were made in Norway, two in Bergen and two in Oslo. This gang comprised of an international selection of suspects: Marco Campas aka Pedro Carbajal Rojas from Peru, Vera Maria Caldas Lima from Brazil, Hernandez Alcalde, from Spain and Mary Eanswide Sulamit Almeida from London. How long the gang was working is unknown, but Interpol was alerted in the summer of 1971, around six months after the Isdal affair. One of the gang was arrested in Düsseldorf, seemingly not part of the four in Norway. This man had 148 fake checks and claimed that the money had been handed up the chain to a Greek.

The four were found guilty on a staggering 60 counts of check fraud in July of 1974. Campas/Rojas and Alcalde were sentenced to four and a half years each for their part in the affair, Sulamit got four years, and Caldas received a sentence of two and half years for pleading guilty. Police, however, suspected they were just one part of a much more extensive criminal network with the leaders based in Italy. The suspects were all given their checks by a man known only as "Albert" in Rome. They were all said to be in fear of the man. It is worth remembering that the most used letter in the woman's notebook as a destination was "R," believed to possibly be Rome.

Organized crime groups active in Rome at the time include the Pesciaroli and, a little later, the Banda della Magliana. Further afield in the Campania region, the likes of the Camorra have extensive links to South America and, in particular, Peru. The 'Ndrangheta of Calabria has developed extensive links throughout South America thanks to the drug trade but restricted their Italian operations to their home region until the mid-1970s. However, they were famed for the kidnapping of John Paul Getty III in 1973, the event taking place in Rome. The scale and scope of the most infamous Italian criminal network, the Cosa Nostra, needs no introduction. The Mafia has a long history of being involved in both smuggling and money scams, with the group investing capital and offering protection to gangs, locally and internationally. The Mafia themselves rarely get directly involved, which would tie with the belief of Asbjørn Bryhn.

However, another clan may be more intriguing. Coincidentally founded in 1970, the Casamonica Clan is lately central to organized crime in Rome. They have their origins with the Romani Sinti tribe and are closely related to the Manouche Romani of France. They speak their own language, which exhibits a strong German influence, and the major Sinti communities are primarily based in Germany. On November 26, 1935, the Nazis declared that the Nuremberg laws applied to gypsies as well as jews, and they lost their rights to citizenship.

Interestingly, the Isdal Woman was consistently noted to be darker-skinned with an exotic appearance that made her stand out in Norway, not to mention Roman Catholic. However, as with Jewish communities, the Sinti were insular, and their strain of Northwestern Indian DNA is therefore usually unquestionably recognized, likely ruling out such a link. Equally, during the war, there were arrests and deportations in Belgium and France of those deemed undesirable. There is also no evidence that any of Rome's organized crime families were at work in Scandinavia during this period. The four arrested for check fraud in 1974 all had Hispanic origins, which the Isdal Woman did not. However, before the Nazis, there was a large Sinti community around Nuremberg.

Isdalen in Bergen, Norway. Reinhardheydt, Wikimedia Commons, public domain.

There is also the possibility that the Isdal Woman's work was nothing criminal or nefarious. She used aliases as perhaps she feared an abusive husband or wished to disappear for other personal reasons. There are many such jobs which would require extensive travel, occupying hotels and living out of a suitcase. The striking good looks of the Isdal Women and liking for the fashion of Paris and Rome may suggest fashion work, with models frequently living nomadic lifestyles and called across borders at a moment's notice. While at 5 foot 4 or 5 and 124lbs, she's a little shorter and heavier than the models of the 1960s; not all models work on the runway, with photographer's models and booth work being typical. However, if the Isdal Women was older than always believed, this may not be realistic, yet the fashion industry is far broader than merely the models. Perhaps also she may have been an artist or a travel writer, any notes or drawings possibly incinerated close to the body.

However, likely, the truth may not be far from the lies. The Isdal Woman spoke German, English, Belgian, and French and claimed to be Belgian. We know she grew up in that region, and if she'd lived there since she was a child, she probably considered herself to be from that country. That doesn't mean she lived in Belgium at the time of her death, yet there is a basis in reality. Using an alias, she needed to at least carry it off when challenged, and having told several witnesses she worked in antiques, it seems likely this was an area she knew well. Perhaps she worked as an agent for an individual or company, representing them at auctions across Europe, for example. The likes of Sotheby's and Christie's in London have regular auctions of antiques and fine art, and there are noted auction houses in all the major cities such as Paris and Rome.

However, if the Isdal Woman had a regular job, nobody ever came forward to say they had worked with her as a client or colleague, despite the massive press the story generated across Norway. Instead, it seems likely her business was something nobody wanted to talk about, work that involved only a few people, or her travels were never work-related at all. Nothing related to any profession was found in her suitcases. While she may have had a job of work usually, there's also the possibility that she had taken time off for her trips around Europe.

Many years ago, it may have seemed that the Isdal Woman was destined to forever lay in her unmarked grave at Bergen, with the possibility of identification remote. However, the advance of modern technology has brought new insight into the deceased's origins, if not any new answers as to what happened that fateful November day in Ice Valley. While the theories of spies and the KGB held enough weight for Norwegian intelligence to take an interest, the likelihood of her working for GRU or the Stasi seems remote when stepping out of the world of Cold War thrillers. She made too many mistakes for that and, despite the ongoing mystery, was too conspicuous. Yet, the fact remains that the deceased did travel all across Europe at somebody's expense, seemingly with a very distinct purpose. Therefore, it seems logical that a sizeable number of people know exactly who she was and why she died. None of them have ever come forward.

We don't know who was behind the woman's work, nor what it was. Indeed, she may have been independently wealthy and not working at all. The passports and attempts to conceal her identity might suggest it was far from a pleasure trip, indicating something criminal. Yet, that too may even have an innocent explanation, and a mental break or accident must be considered. While the manner of her death suggests murder, suicide can't be discounted and, in all probability, seems more likely. However, it might be suggested that a tragic mishap fits many of the facts even more than suicide does. The location was an unlikely place to take a captive for execution. Equally, the method used is overtly complicated when a swift bullet to the head would serve any intelligence agency or criminal gang much better. While the KGB used poisons, these are more familiarly cyanide or ricin, not unsuitable sedatives.

Just because the Isdal Woman may have lived a criminal life, that doesn't mean she died an unlawful death, and we must consider the possibility that there is nothing more profound than our own imaginations.

As mentioned, there is little objective evidence of espionage, nor prostitution, or even any other criminality. Nor that the Isdal Woman was suffering from any mental illness beyond reported anxiety. These theories are built around preconceived notions of an attractive woman traveling around Europe alone being suspicious. They are made on unverified claims of false passports and the "odd" presence of wigs when in truth, there was only one. These phantom wigs are presumed to be disguises when the likelihood exists she may have worn a wig for medical reasons. Equally, the drugs she was carrying were likely for the anxiety, as mentioned earlier, but equally, there is circumstantial evidence this was actually for seizures.

These notions are built on the belief that a single woman talking to random men at hotels must be a prostitute or working for the Soviet Union. This is likely to be an everyday experience for many women, and she was probably the focus of unwanted attention. Is it any wonder many witnesses described her as not wanting to talk? The theories are built on tropes rather than facts, with many witness statements clearly being false. Yet, the peculiarity of the case cannot be denied, nor the obvious questions surrounding the manner of her death. Labels being removed from clothing could simply be more evidence of skin irritation, yet that doesn't explain labels rubbed off bottles. The lack of the eight passports may suggest they didn't really exist, yet is it likely that hotel staff were lax eight times?

When all is said and done, nobody truly knows the truth of the Isdal Woman, and there are questions and speculation at every turn. Facts have become interspersed with myth, and the very real death of a woman has even become fodder for television drama. Something drove her to travel through Europe; there was a purpose there. There was a purpose to her hiding her identity. For somebody, there may have been a purpose to her death. 50 years on from that death, the Isdal Woman remains as intriguing as ever, with only a little more known than the day she was buried in an unmarked grave at Bergen. However, modern techniques look to be moving the balance of probability in favor of identifying the woman and, with only 50 years of history in-between, there may even be suspects still alive if murder is genuinely the case.

No matter who the Isdal Woman was, be it an escort, a terrorist, an international criminal, or even a KGB agent, like all human beings, she deserves better than being left in the cold unknown with nobody to mourn her passing. To the world, she is the mysterious "Isdal Woman;" to others, she is a sister, friend, or lover who vanished long ago. They deserve the truth, and the woman of Ice Valley deserves to finally be given a name.

11 THE MURDER OF CATRINE DA COSTA AND THE SHOW TRIAL THAT FOLLOWED

Sweden, 1984

There are many types of murder and many differing reactions to the circumstances surrounding them. While all killings go rightfully condemned, some go beyond this natural reaction and bring about feelings of extreme revulsion and disgust. These crimes are those that stand out for their brutality and the callousness of the criminal behind them. One such murder is that of Catrine da Costa. The killing is so horrific that it opened up new discourse in Sweden about the way women were treated, being the inspiration behind the publication of Steig Larsson's famous *The Girl with the Dragon Tattoo*, entitled *Men Who Hate Women* in Sweden. The case is one where the value of truth seemingly abandoned Sweden, with no justice to be found for Catrine nor the two men accused of her murder.

Catrine da Costa was born on June 19, 1956, and worked as a prostitute in Stockholm. She had tragically become addicted to heroin while still in high school and became homeless soon afterward. To fund her habit, da Costa turned to prostitution. Her life had almost turned around in 1979 when she moved to Portugal and married a local man, the couple having a son together. However, she couldn't kick her addiction to heroin, and she was sent back to Sweden, being forced again to work at Malmskillnadsgatan in the red light district. She was attractive, dark-haired, and freckled, yet with the ravages of the drugs beginning to show on her young face. By 1984 her habit was getting worse, and to fund her increasing needs, she turned to accepting clients known to be dangerous. It was sometime during the Pentecost celebrations of June 10, 1984, a public holiday in Sweden, that Catrine would disappear, being last seen when she exited a man's vehicle in the red-light area. Her mother raised the alarm after not hearing from her, and every parents' worst nightmare would soon be confirmed.

On July 18, parts of a dismembered body were discovered underneath a bridge at Karlberg's beach in Solna, just north of the Stockholm City Centre. They were dumped in a bin bag. Other body parts were discovered on August 7. Strands of hair and a blue towel were found alongside the bag containing the remains at the scene. Nobody knew how long it had been there. The body was identified as belonging to da Costa through fingerprints, and the condition of the remains meant that no cause of death could be ascertained. Her head, internal organs, one breast, and her genitalia were never recovered.

The media and public were outraged at the circumstances of the crime. While the killing of prostitutes is not unknown in the country, the bloody and visceral horror of the dismemberment, coupled with the callous discarding of the remains as if trash, led to an outpouring of anger from the media, campaigners, and activists alike. Feminist campaigners organized rallies and protests against violence, circulating petitions and making regular television appearances following the killing. The pressure for results was undoubtedly now on Stockholm Police.

Soon after the remains were discovered, eyes turned toward a pathologist at the Department of Forensic Medicine at the Karolinska Institute, the first set of remains being found close by. Dr. Teet Härm was known to use prostitutes and view violent pornography, being considered "creepy" by former colleagues. He sent unsolicited autopsy reports to his friends, complete with graphic photographs, and even invited these friends to watch him perform autopsies. Despite this, he was seen as one of the upcoming lights in his field, already being widely published at 30 years of age and speaking at several international conferences. His specialization was strangulation, and he was considered an expert on sexual violence.

Two years before the killing of Catrine da Costa, Härm's wife, Ann-Catherine, had been found hanged in their bedroom. While the case had at the time been ruled a suicide, there was some suspicion by police working on the matter that it may have been a murder. The deceased was dressed for a night out and in the process of divorcing her husband. Ann-Catherine had been found hanging from the side of their bed with a ligature around her neck. Just two months later, Härm published his first paper on strangulation. Police noted that he seemed unusual and callous after his wife's death, being seen as cold and arrogant by many in his life. However, given the nature of his work, it is not unreasonable to suggest he may have assumed a detached persona, and his personal manner should have no bearing on the facts of the case. The matter officially remained a suicide.

The nature of the dismemberment led investigators to believe a medical man was involved, with Härm's supervisor Jovan Rajs concluding that the killer was skilled in human dismemberment rather than animal dismemberment, ruling out the possibility of a butcher or other animal worker. Härm was arrested after Ann-Catherine's father reported his suspicions to the police. Showing his photo around the red light district, 50 separate women recognized him, with one saying he had been violent toward her. He lied about how often he used prostitutes during questioning, claiming there had only been one incident, while interviews in the red light district suggested otherwise. Despite suspicions, no physical evidence linking him to the crime was found, and he was released five days later. Later that year, he would attempt suicide, losing much of his hearing in the process. While he was not named in the Swedish press, many knew his identity, and his former mother-in-law, Ann-Catherine's mother, was employed by the tabloid *Expressen*. The newspaper was front and center of the campaign against him, portraying the suspect as akin to Hannibal Lecter.

Catrine da Costa. Public domain.

At this same time, Dr. Thomas Allgen, a General Practitioner, was reported to police by his wife on a seemingly unrelated matter. Allgen's wife Christina accused her husband of child sex abuse, claiming that he had molested their 17-month old daughter. At the time, the Allgens were going through a nasty divorce, and examinations revealed no evidence of molestation. The couple would separate later that year.

There was little movement in the case for some time, it being 1985 before police believed a break had finally come. It was revealed that Teet Härm and Thomas Allgen were partially known to each other, having worked together for 18 months between 1980 and 1981. Allgen allegedly even invited Härm and his then-girlfriend to his home for dinner. Once Christina realized that Härm was the individual being talked about as a suspect in the press, she made a phone call to Stockholm police asking if the man was indeed Härm. They shockingly confirmed it was so. She soon made a new accusation against her now ex-husband, claiming that her daughter was saying she had witnessed a dismemberment. The police concluded that the two men must have been jointly involved in the killing of Catrine da Costa. However, on February 28, 1986, Swedish Prime Minister Olof Palme was assassinated in the street near his central Stockholm home, and all police resources were diverted to the hunt for his killer. The assassination would go unsolved, with thousands of man-hours devoted to the killing.

Further evidence would begin to mount against the pair in the autumn of 1987. The owners of a photo shop close to the Karolinska Institute claimed that in the summer of 1984, two men sought to process a film. They alleged that this film contained images of a corpse first decapitated and then dismembered. They claimed they didn't alert the police as the two men had said the pictures were part of a top-secret investigation. Crucially, they picked out Allgen in a line-up, being less sure of Härm. Police believed they had enough evidence to convict the two men on a murder charge, and they were arrested in October. They went to trial in January of 1988.

The trial of Härm and Allgen was a media sensation. The killing had already drawn broad interest and revulsion, and the indictment against two respectable middle-class doctors only added to the public furor. The prosecution alleged that the two men murdered her in the laboratory at the Karolinska Institute before cutting her up using the facilities usually used for forensic medicine. However, the defense contended that the evidence of a child who had been 18-months-old at the time was unsafe, with Allgen's ex-wife having "interpreted" what she was initially being told and child psychologists having behaved unethically afterward. The mother is quoted as saying her child told her at the time that "they threw the head away.. and then the lady was chopped up."

However, the evidence of Allgen's daughter was not the total of the case against him and Härm, with the photograph shop owners giving evidence alongside other witnesses that placed Härm in the company of da Costa. One stated that they had seen both men together with the child at the Department of Forensic Medicine, despite the two men claiming not to have seen each other for two years. Why Allgen would take his daughter to a murder and attempt to develop a film containing evidence was not explained, with these hardly seeming to be the actions of two knowledgeable individuals. Working at a laboratory, Härm would have almost certainly have had private photographic facilities he could have utilized had the men been seeking a trophy.

However, primarily from the evidence of Thomas Allgen's then 5-year-old daughter, both Härm and Allgen were found guilty of killing Catrine da Costa.

There was a feeling amongst many that the integrity of the trial had given way to activist pressure and the sensationalism of the tabloid press. This would have dire consequences when jurors were interviewed in the Swedish daily newspaper *Aftonbladet*, commenting on the court's decisions. The High Court had no choice but to declare a mistrial, both suspects being free to go. The decision was portrayed as another example of men getting away with violence, others suggesting that their social status and well-placed links had ensured they walked away. Public and media pressure once again came to bare and a second trial was arranged.

At the second trial, the Swedish National Board of Health and Welfare was tasked with ascertaining the victim's cause of death. Given the poor condition of the remains, they couldn't say with 100% certainty that Catrine da Costa had indeed been murdered. While the press would portray the decision as absurd given the dismemberment, it is essential to remember that the balance of justice rests on a verdict being beyond a reasonable doubt. With no actual evidence the victim had been murdered, Härm and Allgen were acquitted of the murder charge. At the same time, the judge believed the testimony of Allgen's daughter, finding the duo had indeed dismembered her body.

The statute of limitations on this charge had already expired.

The consequences of the trial wouldn't end there for Härm and Allgen, with both men barred from practicing medicine in May of 1989. Successive appeals by the duo to the Supreme Court of Sweden, the Supreme Administrative Court of Sweden, and the European Court of Human Rights failed to overturn the ruling. Compensation claims from the pair have also been dismissed. The trial's outcome would divide Sweden, with many believing that the two men got away with murder. However, subsequent years and new investigations by the press and crime writers have led most to now think that the entire indictment had been the worst miscarriage of justice ever seen in Scandinavia.

There was never a single piece of physical evidence to fit either man to the crime, and much of the suspicion seems to have been fuelled by personal vendettas. That being from the family of Härm's deceased wife Ann-Catherine and the wife of Allgen. These accusations, coupled with political activism and sordid details of the men's private life, in particular, Härm's frequenting of prostitutes and "creepy" nature, caused a perfect storm of a media sensation, creating a sense of hysteria and moral panic around the case that ended in a show trial. Indeed, the main piece of evidence against the men was based on the testimony of a five-year-old child that many believe had been unduly led by her mother, creating false memory syndrome. Scientists widely accept that individuals can carry false memories and the role of external influence in their formation.

Often left out of retellings is claims from Allgen's ex-wife that his daughter had also spoken of ritual murder, cannibalism, homosexual intercourse, and grilling of heads, suggesting other doctors were also involved in a conspiracy and cult. These fantastical claims are seemingly influenced by widespread moral panics in the 1980s surrounding Satanic ritual abuse, the majority of which has since been widely debunked. Tape recordings of conversations with the child reveal that she said nothing which would independently be considered an accusation, with her responses being interpreted by her mother. Following the case, Allgen was separated from his child permanently.

An expert on the case, Professor Lennart Sjöberg of Stockholm University, told *The Telegraph* that "The child was only 18 months old when she was supposed to witness the cutting up, and yet she was supposed to be able to, some two years later, give credible evidence to child psychologists that is used against the doctors in court? Unbelievable."

The widely respected author and head of research at the Swedish National Police Board, Leif GW Persson, agrees that the two men were innocent. Persson has advised the police for forty years and was involved in the Catrine da Costa killing from the beginning. Speaking to *Metro Mode*, he would describe the investigation as "one of the worst murder investigations I have seen."

"When I first heard about the case and the apprehension of Teet Härm, I was skeptical," Persson told *The Telegraph*. "I spent thousands of hours studying this investigation, and I am convinced that both the doctors accused are innocent. There is no evidence whatsoever. [The investigation was run by] lousy and biased cops, and the media was running berserk."

In 2005, police DNA tested the towel that had been found close to the second dumpsite. Hairs on the article were proven to have not come from either of the two doctors. In 2009, police officially suspended the investigation into the murder of Catrine da Costa, with 25 years having passed since the crime was committed and the statute of limitations now being up.

With most now agreeing that Härm and Allgen were innocent, speculation about who was truly responsible has focused on one man, Stanislaw Gonerka. In 1984, Gonerka was recently released from a mental institution, and his name was discovered in da Costa's diary. He had been seen with prostitutes in Stockholm around the time of the killing, with many saying they were fearful of him. Gonerka was a butcher, and in 1974 he had been sentenced to prison for the murder of a young woman. He strangled her before dismembering the body and discarding the remains in bin bags; the head was never found. Gonerka died in 1987.

While Stanislaw Gonerka seems a good fit for the murder of Catrine da Costa, the case remains officially unsolved. It is likely to be little comfort to

Härm, Allgen, or the family of Catrine da Costa. The focus on the two suspects based on little evidence more than gossip, false witness, and public distaste for them personally, likely allowed a brutal murderer to walk free. Fueled by the tabloid press and political pressure, the investigation, and justice system lost all sense of impartiality and detachment, creating a witch-hunt-like atmosphere that destroyed two of Stockholm's most promising medical professionals' lives and careers, alongside leaving a family without proper justice.

To this day, claims exist online that Härm and Allgen were members of a Satanic cult, that they murdered many more women, and that they engaged in cannibalism and even vampirism. Consistently denied compensation or to be allowed to work again, the case is one where there was no justice for anyone involved. It will remain one of the darkest and most shameful affairs in Swedish criminal history.

12 THE BRUTAL SLAYING OF STINE GEISLER

Denmark, 1990

Murder is a horrific crime in any case. Somebody's life is taken, and the years of experience, knowledge, relationships, and emotions generated by that person become no more in the blink of an eye. Wives, husbands, parents, and children are all deprived of a person who they love. Yet, as we saw with the killing of Catrine da Costa, it is inescapable that some murders provoke feelings of disgust and revulsion more than others. Often that is the murder of the defenseless, of the elderly or children, or where a woman can offer little resistance to a powerful and perverted man.

It is now over thirty years since the brutal killing of Anne Stine Geisler, one such murder that shocked Danish society. The nature of the crime, including evidence of sadism and torture, makes horrific reading.

Anne Stine Geisler seemingly had her entire life in front of her. Intelligent and stunningly attractive, the 18-year-old was studying political science at Denmark's Aarhus University. She had become acquainted with Crown Prince Frederik during her time at the prestigious Krebs School, an institution popular with the upper classes and royalty. Frederik was deeply shaken by events to come, with Geisler's father having also been Prince Frederik's math teacher. The prince is regularly invoked concerning the case by the tabloid press, despite not being seen as a close friend or suspect. The two graduated to different high schools.

Stine was well-liked and popular, being described as both happy and thoughtful. However, on June 4, 1990, she would go missing while walking home from Copenhagen's extensive Pentecost celebrations. In Denmark, these celebrations are the third biggest during the year. They are celebrated over two days — *Pinsedag* (Whit Sunday) and *2. Pinsedag* (Whit Monday). Geisler had been attending a friend's birthday party the same night, with some of the group deciding to travel to a carnival in Copenhagen's city center around midnight. It was rainy, and Geisler bicycled all the way there. By 2am, she decided to head home and took her bicycle, taking a route along the canal at Gammel Strand.

"She was a shining creature. She was fun-loving and with a huge interest in the outside world," Stine's mother, Kirsten, told *New Idea*. "I still don't understand who could hurt my beloved daughter."

Stine lived in an apartment above her parents in the Teglgårdsstræde region of the city and had an agreement that she would post a note through their door to say she had returned home safe. The message never came. When Stine couldn't be found the following day for a planned family lunch in South Zealand, her parents began frantic calls to friends, family, and acquaintances, and around 6pm that same day, their desperation would have a tragic ending. A chef entered the basement of the building, regularly using the space as a changing room for her work at a restaurant situated on the ground floor. There, she discovered the body of Geisler.

The body was fully clothed, wearing the same cognac-colored leather coat, short skirt, yellow stockings, and burgundy-colored shoes as the previous evening. Stine had her hands tied behind her back with a black cord, the rope also looping around her neck and connected to a door handle; if she had moved, she would have been strangled. Her face and neck also featured several incisions made with either a knife or shards of glass. Two dishrags were stuffed in her mouth. On her arm, what appeared to be the letters "PK" had been cut into the skin. A pack of condoms lay underneath the woman, and bone wax had been poured all over the body. Despite the presence of the condoms, no evidence of rape or sexual assault was found.

An autopsy subsequently concluded that Stine had died of suffocation after the dishcloths had pressed her tongue down her own throat, cutting off her air supply. Police believe that Geisler was surprised by the killer and dragged down to the basement where he improvised, the rope and other instruments used in the killing having already been found in the basement. Some suggested there may have been a ritual element to the killing, considering the cutting of the arm and the use of bone wax. Others believed the wax was an attempt to remove forensic traces from the scene. A police profile described the killer as a "sadistic and perverted person who enjoys abusing and humiliating women."

Opening a murder inquiry, Danish police quickly discovered that Stine had an eventful private life, frequenting several cafes and bars where she met men and engaged in relationships. The details were meticulously detailed in her diary. The bohemian Sabine's Cafeteria was one such location, a haunt for many actors, filmmakers, writers, and journalists. One relationship she had seemingly developed through the café caught the eye of police, being with a married 40-year-old journalist, a man 22 years her senior. The journalist worked for one of Copenhagen's major morning newspapers. He was quickly brought in for questioning and readily admitted to the relationship. He was dismissed when he presented a watertight alibi for the night in question.

However, he was far from the only man in her life with witnesses saying she'd been in the company of a different man the night before the Pentecost celebrations, arguing with him at Sabine's. Geisler was also seen on the day itself taking lunch with a man at her workplace, Café Wilder. The man was described as young, average-looking, and with short hair and an unshaven face. Again, the man was quickly identified and eliminated from inquiries when it became clear his alibi was solid. He was described variously as both sweet and charming or unpleasant and horrible. He seemed to divide opinion amongst many and lived in the same street as the Geisler family. Yet another man was never identified. A security guard said that he had seen an individual in leather trousers outside the Geisler residence when the victim went missing. Another said that a man matching the same description was loitering outside Christianshavns Gymnasium a few days before Stine was killed.

Police began to move away from the theory that Anne Stine Geisler was killed by an acquaintance and began to suspect she had been killed by a stalker or an opportunistic sex criminal. One suspect began to stand out. Known as "Mr. Smiley," then 28-year-old Peter Kronholm lived at a commune not far from where Geisler was killed and had previous convictions for aggravated assault, abuse, and various frauds. He was questioned several times and had no alibi for his whereabouts after 1am. He also had the initials PK, the same lettering seemingly cut into Stine Geisler's arm and had been seen on the night of the murder at Café Floss, just a short distance from the basement where Stine Geisler was murdered. Following the killing, he moved quickly from the area.

Kronholm would go on to become one of Denmark's most notorious killers. Described as cynical and brutal, he was charming and polite to women he met around Copenhagen, yet also violent, controlling, and a future brothel owner. In 1994, he murdered his girlfriend, Anette Enevoldsen, a young stockbroker.

He had told a web of lies about his life, giving an image of respectability before being exposed. Anette ended the relationship, and an enraged Kronholm beat her with a hammer before strangling her. Two years prior, another girlfriend of Kronholm, Charlotte Machon-Fellov, vanished into thin air. She hasn't been seen since, and "Mr. Smiley" is suspected of her murder. Despite suspicions, police had nothing to link Kronholm to the Stine Geisler crime scene and no real motive, with sexual assault unable to be proven by the pathologist.

In 2003, he was amazingly released on parole and established a brothel at his apartment in the Østerbro area of the city. He employed a receptionist and prostitute to work at the establishment, both living in fear of him. On one occasion, the receptionist went to pick up her salary from his apartment, and Kronholm attacked her. She was handcuffed, had her mouth taped, and was thrown down on a bed. The killer pulled a plastic bag over her head, intending to suffocate her, even tying a rope around her neck. The assault only ended when the victim's phone rang, and it became clear she had a friend waiting just down the road. In 2006, "Mr. Smiley" attempted to murder a witness to one of his other many crimes, blasting him twice with a shotgun after a kidnapping.

Kronholm is almost certainly a serial killer and may be linked to other crimes in Copenhagen during the 1990s. Around the time of the murder, there were five other killings of women in the city, all unsolved. Two of these killings, Edith André in 1987 and Lene Rasmussen in 1990, were attributed to serial rapist Marcel Hansen, aka the Amager Man, being convicted of the slayings in 2011. Some believe that Hansen is also in the frame for the Stine Geisler killing; however, while the murder of Edith André involved the victim being attacked in her own home, there is little else to suggest a link. Both women were manually strangled by Hansen and had money and jewelry stolen from their person. A subsequent search for DNA on Stine's clothes didn't turn up a match. However, Hansen is noted as using the same unusual wrist-to-neck technique of tying up his victims that was seen in this case.

In all, 4,000 people were questioned about the murder, with the police coming up empty-handed. The affair remained a top priority for police in Copenhagen for years after the killing, with Detective Inspector Ove Dahl leading inquiries, then being the head of homicide. Dahl believes that Hansen is responsible, saying: "I can not prove it, but the suspicion will always be there because he was active in those years.

"It's the ultimate crime. No one has heard or seen anything in the case. But the perpetrator must never have peace. My greatest hope, of course, is that the case will be resolved," said Dahl.

The Detective Inspector believes that the killing was likely an opportunistic attack with a sexual motive, with Stine unlikely to have known her killer whether it was Hansen or not. In 2012, it was reported that police had succeeded in obtaining a DNA profile of the murderer, bringing suspicion on both Hansen and Kronholm into doubt.

"I think Stine Geisler was killed because she was so unlucky," the detective said. "She met a psychopathic power-hungry person who wanted to have a sexual relationship with her through violence and force. It was not just anyone we were looking for."

The murder of Stine Geisler was a killing that shocked Copenhagen and Denmark, the brutality of the killing seeming to suggest a level of confidence and danger that would lead to more crimes in the future. This was likely to be far from a first attack. Those beliefs may have been proven right should either of the two most likely suspects, Kronholm and Hansen, be responsible. However, while both are heavily suspected, there are positives and negatives with both theories. While Hansen was known to tie his victims the same way as Geisler, his other crimes bear little similarity. While Kronholm's violence against women is apparent, and he shares the initials seemingly carved into Stine's arm, his known and suspected killings are of women he knew personally, often in a fit of rage. However, it seems likely that Kronholm is the best fit for the crime, not only being in the near vicinity at the time but moving away in haste afterward.

The possibility exists, however, that a killer may have slipped entirely under the radar, never being looked at for the crime. The murder has unique features, none of which have seemingly been repeated in any other crime. While it may have been a single killing, the perpetrator satisfied, incarcerated, or dead, that seems unlikely. He will have struck again. With other killings from the period still unsolved, the potential that a serial killer got away and continues to stalk the streets

of Copenhagen is the fear that overshadows the
entire case.

13 THE DISAPPEARANCE AND LIKELY MURDER OF HELENA ANDERSSON

Sweden, 1992

All of the cases highlighted in this collection features the murder of women. From those killed in their own homes to those murdered on vacation, it appears that women are not safe from men the world over. However, there is one form of crime that every woman fears, that being the attack in the dark while walking home. There are numerous cases of such killings, not just in the Nordic countries, with the lack of lighting and witnesses turning any street, alley, or park into the hunting grounds of a predator.

Where our last two cases horrified for the brutality of the killings, our following case is horrific for a whole other reason, that being the ability of somebody who wants us gone to make us vanish into thin air. Combining the two, the case of Helena Andersson is possibly one of the most creepy in the annals of Swedish crime.

Helena Andersson was 22 years old and carefree, her whole life seemingly ahead of her. However, that would all change on June 14, 1992, a hot summer's day in Mariestad, a small town of around 15,000 in North-East Sweden. Helena had been out dancing with friends at a local hotel, enjoying herself. Tired, she was ready to come home and phoned shortly before closing to tell her sister she had forgotten her keys. During the same phone call, her sister insisted Helena get a taxi. However, she never came home. The next day, police searching the area for the young woman came across the only trace they ever found — her sandals laying in a pasture and her rings alongside the road Helena would have walked. They were a mere 100 yards from the home she shared with her parents.

"I have a life before and a life after Helena disappeared," said Helena's sister. "I have never really been able to feel an unconditional joy for anything, or really able to ever feel anything anymore."

The last confirmed sighting of Helena was in a square, with several witnesses having spoken to her. From here, her movements are unknown, with a taxi station being 300 yards away and several exits she could have taken if on foot. Equally, she may have been willingly picked up in a car. Some have contended that she was snatched from the square, yet this was a pleasant summer night, and the area was full of potential witnesses. None reported seeing anything of that nature, suggesting that Helena either willingly went home in a taxi or private vehicle or simply walked.

Despite the lack of a body, the police investigation into the case was treated as a murder inquiry from the very beginning. An early witness statement said that a dog walker heard the desperate screams in the area on the night in question. The witness, who had been known to Helena for about 20 years, walked her dog between 2:10am, and 2:30am. She states that she first heard a commotion coming in the direction of Ekuddenvägen. Moving onto the bicycle path, she then listened to the screams, saying they came from an area toward Helena's home, perhaps a playground situated close by. The cries lasted for around five minutes, and there were two male voices present, both Swedish. Despite the cries, described as despair rather than terror or fright, there was no call for help. The witness states that "Helena" was shouting out "no, no" and "you mustn't do that." The noise ended with the loud slamming of a car door, but the witness heard no engine driving away. She was 100% certain it was Helena she heard shouting with no possibility she may have been mistaken. Another witness meanwhile said they observed a white car, possibly a Honda, driving around the streets near Helena's home. This vehicle passed by her house twice and had no headlights on.

There was certainly no shortage of leads in the case, with plenty of rumors and innuendo to suggest what fate had befallen Helena. Some believe it was a clear case of a rogue taxi driver picking up Helena and driving her away against her will. Some suggested a teacher was involved. Many years Helena's senior, the teacher was already married and had allegedly gotten Helena pregnant. Frightened of his infidelity being exposed, he had killed Helena. Others claimed that there was all manner of dodgy characters working as doormen at the hotel, with one later being convicted in 1998 of the murder of a taxi driver. *Perception of Murder*, a documentary by Kanal 5, suggested she'd ended up hidden in an aviation fuel tank.

There were three main suspects in the case in the 1990s, identified only as "The 25-Year Old", "The Detainee," and "The Man in the Pilot Glasses." The Detainee was already known to Helena, and at the time of the disappearance, he was living outside Skaraborg. Several tips sent to police raised suspicions about the man, and when questioned by a journalist, he said cryptically that he knew "someone who was in Mariestad that night." The Detainee was brought in for questioning in 1996, spending two nights in custody. Police subsequently concluded he had nothing to do with the disappearance and removed him from the inquiry.

"The 25-Year-Old" was the first man arrested in connection with the disappearance of Helena, being detained in July 1992, just over a month afterward. The primary evidence held against the man was that a witness claimed he had seen Helena entering the man's car on the night that she went missing, police finding white dog hair on the vehicle's backseat. Helena also owned a white dog. However, the witness statement was entirely false and malicious, with the offender sentenced to prison for making up the incident. There is no suggestion that the 25-Year-Old had been involved in the disappearance in any way at all.

That leaves one main suspect and the best lead that still remains in the case, "The Man in the Pilot Glasses." Before closing time, Helena had been seen with a man wearing distinctive aviator-style sunglasses at the hotel. The individual stayed till just before Helena left on the night of her disappearance. His appearance would match that of a man that a witness says he saw in the company of a woman headed toward the Andersson's home. While the witness couldn't be sure the woman was Helena, a description of her trousers matches those worn at the time of her vanishing. He quickly became one of the primary suspects in the case after it was revealed that he had no strong alibi for the time after the hotel's closing; this was coupled with his story constantly "swaying," according to investigators. However, in 2019 prosecutors revealed that the man is no longer considered a suspect in the case, noting that with no evidence of murder, the statute of limitations has expired on any other potential charge.

The investigation into the suspected murder is still ongoing, however, and in 2018, investigators sent the sandals and rings for analysis at the National Forensic Center (NFC). The results showed three different traces: a mixed match and the others being separate hits for a man and a woman. The woman showed a familial match for Helena and can be discounted; however, the man was harder to identify, with nothing in the NFC database. There was no DNA found on the ring. Investigators quickly pointed out that while none of the DNA on Helena's sandals matched the

"Man in the Pilot Glasses," that didn't rule him out of inquiries, with no evidence those profiles were linked to the crime.

Gothenburg's Cold Case group has since taken over the matter, seeking to shed some new light on the affair that most people believe to be a murder. The group is staffed by six officers who dedicate their time to continuing the investigations of cases considered cold. With the new DNA evidence being on the table, all be it with disappointing results, many are pleased that the police seem to once again be moving forward on a matter that has perplexed Sweden for over 28 years.

"Now it feels a bit like they have actually taken in what we say and want and that there is a strong will that we should move forward, sort this out and go to the finish line," says Helena's sister.

It seems possible that Helena was kidnapped in a vehicle, either while walking home or from the hotel itself. She could undoubtedly have phoned a taxi or hailed one in the street, falling victim to a predator in a fake cab as so many others have before and since. Equally, she may have called a friend for a lift home, that friend having other intentions than providing a service. Had Helena been transported in a vehicle, then her body could conceivably be anywhere, even in someone's back garden.

However, eyewitness statements seem to suggest Helena was on foot, one reporting having seen somebody matching her description and yet another hearing screams from around the woods. These screams were noted by somebody familiar with Helena and, intriguingly, didn't seem to be cries for help. However, if Helena was on foot, this poses the problem of what happened to the body? It is rare for an opportunistic rapist or killer to go to the trouble of expertly hiding a body after an attack. Equally, while Helena's sandals would likely fall off in a struggle, the rings are harder to explain. Located by a road, they were possibly thrown from a car. Were these rings offensive to the perpetrator? Was it a robbery gone wrong? Did she throw them herself as a clue? All questions that sadly have no answers.

In 2021, nearly 30 years after Helena went missing, there was a significant breakthrough in the case when a Mariestad man was arrested on suspicion of murder. The suspect, in his 60s, had previously appeared in the investigation but never as a suspect. Investigators subsequently cordoned off a residence on Dragspelsvägen in Radbyn as searched the property with a dog team. They did not comment on what the search was for.

The man, who denied the allegations, was said by acquaintances to be a loner who has had mental illness since the early 1990s. He had owned a car similar to the one seen in the area on the night of Helena's disappearance, yet police believe the vehicle was scrapped long ago.

The case is ongoing, and at the time of publishing, the suspect is still in custody.

14 THE MYSTERIOUS DEATH OF THE OSLO WOMAN

Norway, 1995

On June 3, 1995, a young woman was found dead at the Plaza Hotel in Oslo, Norway. She had been shot once through the head, the pistol in her hand indicating a clear case of suicide. Indeed, that's exactly what the death was ruled. However, in a case with eerie echoes of the Isdal Woman, all the labels were removed from her clothing. There were whispers of organized crime and international espionage at every turn. 26 years later, investigators may be about to find out the truth behind the woman in Room 2805, putting an end to one of the biggest mysteries in the history of Norwegian crime.

The Radisson SAS Plaza Hotel, now known as the Radisson Blu Plaza Hotel, is a towering landmark in the Norwegian capital, standing 384 ft in height as the country's second-tallest building. It had been completed in 1989 and was the epitome of a modern five-star hotel, with 1,500 beds in 673 rooms across 37 floors. Millionaires, international stars, and both the rich and famous stayed at the Raddison. In 1995, Room 2805 would become possibly the most infamous of them all.

It was just after 7:30pm when a receptionist at the Plaza named Evy Tudem Gjertsen became aware something was wrong in 2805. The room was registered to two Belgians, Jennifer and Lois Fairgate, and their credit card had seemingly exceeded the limit. The business-class room was located in what was called "the tower." It was one of the best at the Radisson, costing around $330 per night in current monetary terms, and, having stayed three nights, the occupants had not paid a dime, despite messages on previous days. How somebody managed to stay in the hotel without prepaying or providing payment guarantees has never been explained. Yet, the lack of diligence by some members of staff has been noted by witnesses.

"It's incomprehensible to me," former Plaza Hotel receptionist Tudem Gjertsen said to *Verdens Gang*. "We had strict routines at the hotel. It just shouldn't be possible."

Gjertsen did precisely as she was trained to do and sent a message to the room via the TV screen asking for somebody to contact the cashier. The system was controlled by the remote control for the television, and somebody acknowledged receipt by pressing the OK button.

Outside Room 2805. Oslo Police photo.

Gjertsen wasn't satisfied, however. After conversing with other staff, she discovered the room hadn't been cleaned since Thursday, and a "do not disturb" sign had been posted on the door. She decided to call security, and soon enough, security guard Espen Næss arrived at Room 2805. As he knocked on the door, a noise echoed from within, and Næss realized at once it had been a gunshot. Taking cover in a small alcove, the security guard waited it out, fearing the second occupant of the room was armed and had opened fire on the other. He didn't relay any of this information to other staff, despite believing an active shooter was in the building. Næss didn't want to cause a panic and instead went back down to the guard station, leaving the room completely unwatched.

The head of security was quickly alerted, and the police called. The superior tried to get a response at the door, having made his own way up to the room. There was no response. He opened the door, which was locked from inside, and noted a bad smell. What that smell was is not known, though it was likely propellant and the "smell of death," including blood and body fluids. The place was dark, yet on the bed, he could make out the form of a woman in a position that seemed unnatural. The security man called out to no response. Realizing she was dead, he exited and waited for the police to arrive. It was around 8:05pm, and the police arrived 50 minutes later.

Upon investigating, the police found the victim to have suffered a massive gunshot wound to the forehead, undoubtedly killing her instantly. There was significant blood splatter in the room and on the bed. There were no signs of anyone else being present. The gun, believed to be a Browning 9mm, still rested in her hands. It was unusually positioned, with the thumb on the trigger. It had been fired twice, once into a pillow as a test shot and once more into the woman's head. While CSI combed the room for clues and other statements were made privately, it seemed that the case was a tragic suicide. Both keycards were inside the room, and the door had been double-locked, meaning that only security had access. The window was open but, 28 floors from the ground, it was unlikely to have been an entry or exit point. Subsequent reports all agreed, the woman had committed suicide. The hotel's own internal report stated that it was "99.9 percent certain" that she had taken her own life.

The positioning of the body on the bed. Oslo police photo.

However, that 0.1% of doubt seems to be a lot more critical than anyone wished to admit. While everything indeed points to the fact that the Oslo Plaza Woman was alone in the room, there are oddities. For example, there was no gunshot residue on her hands, nor any blood. The serial number of the gun had been expertly removed with acid. 25 rounds of ammunition were found in her bag and nothing else. All her clothing tags had been removed, a feature reminiscent of the infamous Isdal Woman case. And, just like in the older death, nobody had any idea who the victim was.

Torleiv Ole Rognum, a professor of forensic medicine and Norway's most senior forensic medical expert, told *Verdens Gang* that he thought it "odd" that "there was no back spatter or singeing on her hands."

"That is really unusual. We know there was a powerful back spatter with blood way up on the ceiling. The victim still had her thumb on the trigger and her fingers around the grip," said Rognum. "It's strange there is no blood trace on her hands. As a forensics expert, I find that striking.

"I would have expected to find it. Some suicide victims also get scrapes or marks on their fingers from the recoil. In this case, there are no marks on the finger or the trigger. A 9mm pistol gives a powerful recoil."

With the Isdal Woman taking place in 1970, the lack of modern policing methods and technology can be blamed for failures to identify the victim. Not so the Oslo Woman, who seems to have gone to expert lengths not to be identified. Her short black hair may have been an attempt to alter her appearance. There was no passport or purse, no ID cards or documents. There was no credit card. No driver's license. Nothing to give police a clue to where she had come from except the gun being of Belgian manufacture and the fact she had claimed to be from Rue de la Stehde in the village of Verlaine, Belgium. The street doesn't exist. Nor did the company she claimed to work for, "Cerbis." However, the link to Belgium was strengthened through phone records, as she attempted to make two calls to incorrect numbers during her stay. Based on similar working numbers in the area, these calls were to Grâce-Hollogne or Seraing, both neighboring municipalities of Verlaine. It seems she may have simply got the number wrong, suggesting, perhaps, she had written it down incorrectly after being told or had misremembered.

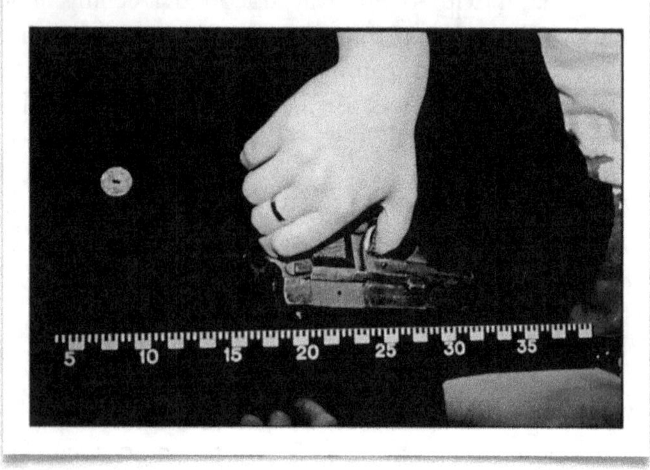

The gun unusually positioned in the hand. Oslo Police photo.

The Browning 9mm is a popular and powerful weapon utilized by police, military, and criminals alike. Millions of the guns are in circulation, and with a shot being fired into a pillow as a muffled test, it seems likely that the mystery woman was unfamiliar with it. Guns are an incredibly unpopular choice for suicides amongst women. However, even the most inexperienced handlers will have known that 25 bullets, plus seven in the magazine, was far more ammunition required for a suicide. Had they belonged to someone else? Or had the dead woman been planning a crime that would have required such firepower?

"There's nothing to suggest this was anything but a suicide," criminal watch commander Lennart Kyrdalen told *Verdens Gang*. "But it is very rare to find a woman who has shot herself. I have never seen it, before or since."

Interestingly, no fingerprints were found on the gun or magazine, but this isn't as suspicious as it sounds, with the lifting of prints from a pistol being the realm of police procedurals and not reality. In truth, getting marks from the surface of a gun is very difficult, and their absence isn't a suggestion that the weapon had been wiped clean. However, it doesn't discount that notion either. If the gun was indeed cleaned, it wouldn't be the only missing evidence from the crime scene.

The manufacturing/laundry labels removed from her clothing were not done to prevent irritation; they were systematically cut away, with even the manufacturer's name on her shoes removed. Only one label remained, that being on a René Lezard jacket that had been sold in Germany. A bag retained the brand of German manufacturer Travelite. Both these labels would have been impossible to remove without destroying the linings of the products.

While René Lezard is not amongst the first rank fashion houses and not overly expensive, the company is noted for its style and shows the woman was concerned for her appearance. Yet, there were no toiletries or makeup in her room beyond an empty bottle of Ungaro's Pour L'Homme 1 cologne. It was for a man. While the possibility exists that the bottle belonged to the man some reported seeing her with, equally, the bottle may never have contained cologne at all. Or, with empty perfume bottles retaining their scent for many years afterward, perhaps the bottle was a reminder of lost love. The only fingerprints on the bottle belonged to the victim.

The autopsy, likewise, turned up little. The coroner ascertained that she was older than she had claimed on hotel documents, being between 25 and 35 rather than 21. She had short black hair and blue eyes, being 5 foot 3 inches tall and weighing 147lbs. Her dental work was expensive, being done in porcelain and gold in a fashion utilized in the United States, Germany, Denmark, and Switzerland. Despite the quality of the work, no dental matches were ever made, and her fingerprints didn't match anyone on record. While the deceased was found to have no alcohol in her system, no tests were done for drugs, and no samples were taken from the fingernails or vagina that might indicate defensive wounds or sexual assault. As mentioned, there was no gunshot residue on the hands or blood.

Despite suicide remaining the primary line of inquiry, Assistant Chief of Police Gunnar Larsen, was not satisfied with the case's many questions. Five homicide detectives were assigned to investigate the circumstances of the mystery woman's death and who exactly she was. Indeed, as late as three weeks after the death, police were still unwilling at that point to definitively say it was a suicide.

"We are not sure if the woman took her own life or if she was eliminated by persons unknown," Assistant Chief of Police Gunnar Larsen said to *Dagbladet*. "All we're sure of is that we have a lot of questions, which the investigation has not yet answered."

Interviewing staff at the Plaza Hotel, police ascertained that the woman had checked in at 10:44pm on May 31 under the name Jennifer Fairgate, incorrectly signing her assumed name as "Fergate." She was asked for no identification and stated that a Lois Fairgate would be staying with her. While the receptionist believed that she was alone, others questioned indicated that they thought they had seen her in the company of a man between the ages of 35 and 40. She spoke English while making her initial booking and, when calling to confirm, spoke German. Investigators found that she had mostly stayed inside her room for the entirety of her stay. This was except for the early morning of June 1 through June 2, when she stayed out between 12:34am, and 8:50am. What she was doing in the middle of the night and the following day has never been ascertained.

A maid at the hotel recalled that she had seen a nice pair of shoes in the closet of Room 2805 during this period of absence, and they were no longer amongst the items thought to belong to the deceased. Indeed, a considerable amount may have been missing from the room, with "Jennifer" found to have a very odd assortment of clothing. These included four jackets but only one blouse. She had one sweater but no trousers or skirts. She had pajama shorts, pantyhose, and four bras but no panties. Equally, the clothing wouldn't fit in the Travelite bag. A witness reported that "Jennifer" had arrived at the Plaza Hotel with a wheeled suitcase and wearing a suit jacket with a skirt, leading her to assume that the victim had been a flight attendant as it was typically airline crews that had this type of luggage at the time. The witness believed she was from British Airways. Neither the suitcase nor the skirt was in the room.

The view into the room. Oslo Police photo.

Retired policeman Tom Storm Olsen would tell *Verdens Gang* he believed "she must have been in a desperate situation," yet "it's hard to say why because we don't know who she was. There may well have been something criminal about it."

"She was an elegant lady. Why did she come to Oslo and check into the Plaza? Was there something else she had in mind doing? We looked into many groups and social backgrounds but found nothing. We thought maybe it was a drug case or that she was supposed to carry out a mission for someone. Lots of police units were involved. If she was sent to kill someone, who was it? We searched but never found any answers… That she went to such lengths to not be identified. That is very unusual."

Police had several theories about who "Jennifer" might be, including the missing wife of a mafia boss. That was quickly debunked. Others believed that it might be a drug matter, with some suspecting the hand of the intelligence services or that the woman was even an assassin. However, all of these ideas quickly fizzled away to nothing, and on June 26, 1996, the Oslo Woman was buried in an anonymous grave at Oslo's Vestre Gravlund Cemetery. Just two months later, the police ordered the destruction and/or sale of all the evidence, including the clothing, jewelry, luggage, and even the gun.

The gun was later found to have been saved, with the police forensics department looking to display a weapon that showed evidence of having its markings removed. The weapon was found by the Norwegian newspaper *Verdens Gang* in 2017 amidst a new investigation by the journalist Lars Christian Wegner who has followed the case since 1998. Experts who contacted Wegner following the finding suggested that the weapon was not an authentic Browning 9mm at all and was, in fact, a Hungarian copy composed of differing parts. While the barrel was genuine, the rest of the gun was likely to be much older than the suggested 1991 date of manufacture. Experts believe it likely had its origin in the 1960s or 1970s, being an ex-military issue.

The gun used to kill the Oslo Woman. Oslo Police photo.

Wegner's subsequent inquiries have highlighted another intriguing factor, that being a man who stayed in Room 2804.

Known publicly only as "Mr. F," the man was Belgian, and at 8:06pm on the day of the death, "Jennifer Fairgate" ordered food to be taken to her room, a "Hotbite" of bratwurst and potato salad. Kristin Andersen, the room service supervisor, brought the food up but had seemingly been given the wrong number, taking the food to 2804 instead of 2805, the room across the corridor. That was occupied by Mr. F. The "mistake" was cleared up, and the mystery woman delivered the food directly opposite. She gave a massive tip of 50-kroner.

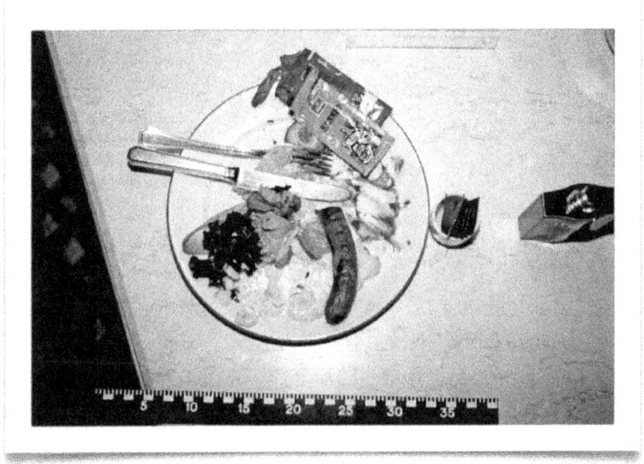

The last meal of the victim. Oslo Police photo.

Crime scene investigators discovered most of the food in the room, with little being eaten, despite it seemingly being the final meal of someone's life. The "mistake" is interesting as it serves to let 2805 know that 2804 is in residence, and while it might be easily dismissed, police also found a *USA Today* newspaper in the dead woman's room. These newspapers had been given free to all guests in the hotel. Only, this wasn't for Room 2805 or 2804 and was, in fact, the newspaper that had been intended for Room 2816. Another mistake, or had the woman been spying on other residents and entering their rooms? A fingerprint was recovered from the bag containing the newspaper and was recently sent to Interpol.

Whoever stayed in 2816 has never been traced.

Police documents show that "Mr. F" was in Oslo for work and was from the French-speaking part of Belgium. He was never questioned as he had already checked out on the morning of the apparent suicide. Lars Christian Wegner attempted to speak to the man as part of his investigations. The individual was hesitant to say anything, cutting off contact when he was informed that journalists wished to discuss the Oslo matter. Insistent, the tenacious Wegner traveled to Belgium and spoke to the man directly.

"I remember it well because they asked me about it at the front desk when I checked out. Someone asked if I had heard or seen anything since it was in the same corridor. But I slept well that night and knew nothing about it...." Mr. F said to *Verdens Gang*. "I stayed there from Friday to Saturday. When I checked out, they told me about the lady who died. I've stayed at thousands of hotels, so for me, this was no big thing."

However, with the suicide happening in the evening, there is no way that the front desk could have informed Mr. F of a death that had not yet happened when he checked out in the morning, a fact confirmed by records. Mr. F hasn't responded to further inquiries by Wegner, and there is no explanation as to why he would lie. Of course, he could simply be mistaken or not wish to get involved.

In November of 2016, there were new developments in the case when the body of the Oslo Woman was exhumed to secure DNA analysis. Blood samples, like the rest of the evidence, had been discarded in 1996.

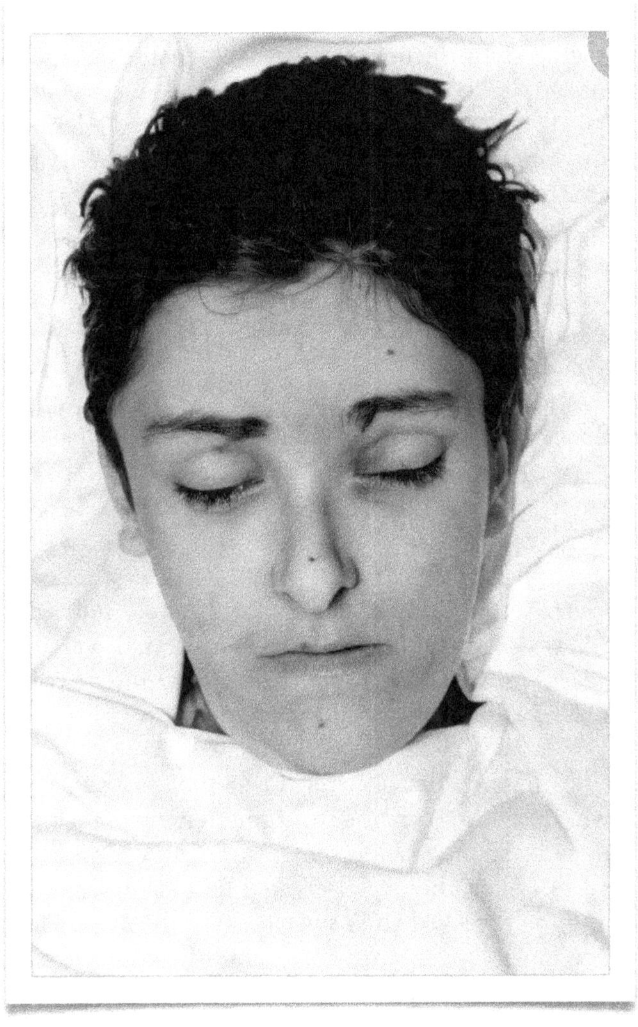

Photo of the deceased Oslo Woman released in an attempt at identification. Oslo police photo.

Investigators took samples of both teeth and bones. They obtained a complete DNA profile, sending the material for analysis at the Institute for Legal Medicine at Innsbruck Medical University, in Austria. The samples confirmed that the Oslo Woman was most likely European. A study of her teeth by Professor Jurian Hoogewerf at the University of Canberra in Australia narrowed the area to Germany. Yet further analysis, this time by Professor Druid in Stockholm, suggests the woman was born in 1971 and was aged 24 at the time of her death, with a small margin of error of just 1.1 years.

The information generated ties with what little evidence was found in the room. As you may recall, the Oslo Woman's jacket and bag were both of German origin, and the woman said to be speaking the language without an accent on the phone to the hotel staff. Her dental work may also have originated in Germany. While she clearly had some knowledge of Belgium, particularly the region around Verlaine, there is no evidence suggesting that the mystery woman was actually from that area.

As the mystery of who the Oslo Woman begins to slowly unravel, so might the actual circumstances of her death. While suicide remains the official position of Oslo Police, the questions that homicide detectives were initially tasked to answer remain unsolved. How, for example, did the woman get into the country? Was she an existing German immigrant, or did she travel to Norway? Was the gun smuggled through customs or bought into the country? What happened to her missing belongings and documents?

One possibility is that the Isdal Woman case directly inspired events in Oslo. As recanted in an earlier chapter, the affair remains Norway's most well-known unsolved case, centering on a mysterious woman who died after being set on fire at Bergen on November 29, 1970. Police at the time judged the matter to be a suicide. Yet, details such as missing clothing tags meant that the mystery lingered. The possibility that the security services were involved has always seemed likely, and neither police nor the public have managed to identify the woman. The case was certainly known in 1995, and somebody wishing to remain anonymous may have taken inspiration from the successful methods utilized by the Isdal Woman.

Like "Jennifer," the Isdal Woman consistently gave her nationality as Belgian when she was actually German, having likely been raised in French-speaking Belgium. The Oslo Woman had expensive gold and porcelain work done on her teeth, while the Isdal Woman also had unique gold-filling dental work. With a +/- 1.1 on the Oslo Woman's year of birth being 1971, she may, in fact, have been born in 1970, the same year the Isdal Woman died. Could it be that the woman in Room 2805 deliberately tried to make her own suicide echo the Isdal Woman? If she was trying to create these false echoes, it would explain the failed calls to Belgium and simple mistakes such as street names.

In the Isdal case, police eventually found her belongings in two suitcases at Bergen railway station. Suppose the Oslo Woman was indeed a partial copycat. In that case, it seems likely that the suitcase missing from the Radisson likely ended up close to

Oslo Central Station, which, coincidentally, is in view of the hotel. Equally, if the echoes had initially been intended greater, she could have traveled to Bergen during the 20 hours she is unaccounted for at the hotel. Bergen is a 7-hour journey by train. Fearful of being found with the gun, she may have ended her plan prematurely.

Copycat suicides, also known as the Werther Effect, are defined as the duplication of suicide methodology from public knowledge of the original act. This knowledge can come from personal or local information or depictions in the news or accounts across books, television, and film. Most cases happen within a short timeframe of the original death, but not universally. This "suicide contagion" is often linked to young people and famous people, such as the suicide of Kurt Cobain or the Japanese musician Hide. It may be possible that the Oslo Woman had become obsessed with the Isdal case, being a copycat. However, this explanation might not account for the presence of the gun. As mentioned, the Isdal Woman burned to death.

As in many cases with mysterious elements and unidentified bodies, the specter of espionage was raised early, with the police said to have entertained the idea before dismissing it. The theory is also prevalent with the Isdal Woman. Removing the labels from garments makes them far harder to trace, and the lack of identifying documents suggests somebody with something to hide. While some tellings of the tale highlight the role the Raddison played in the Oslo Accords between Israel and Palestine, with Yasser Arafat and Yitzhak Rabin signing the document in the

Royal Suite alongside Bill Clinton, these events happened in 1993, some considerable time before the death of "Jennifer Fairgate."

"We had follow-up meetings after the Oslo Agreement both in 1994 and 1995, but not at the end of May/early June," Jan Egeland, then a state secretary in the Ministry of Foreign Affairs, told *Verdens Gang*. "Nor were there other peace talks or processes in that period where tensions were so high that an attack would have been a concern."

Many of these theories fail to understand how the security services actually operate and are based on Cold War fiction instead of fact. Undercover, agents will always guarantee their backstory is watertight, not transparently false as the Oslo Woman's was. They would undoubtedly have ensured they paid for the hotel room so as not to raise suspicion. Equally, they would have had no need to own a firearm said to be a relic of the Cold War, cobbled together as the "Browning" was. And, finally, unless killed in an operation likely to cause a major international scandal, an agent would not be disavowed and left to rest in an anonymous grave had the woman been MI6 or CIA. However, this is not the case for some other services.

While the newspaper from Room 2816 may seem suspicious, it stands at odds with the belief that a killer was thorough enough to make a murder look like a suicide. While Mr. F's behavior and statement are also suspicious, he may simply fear being linked to a potential crime or have his own reasons for not wishing to be in the public eye. One theory, after all, is that "Jennifer Fairgate" may have been a high-class escort.

"Norway, Sweden, and Austria were typical 'safe-havens' where intelligence services could hold meetings and work in peace," Ola Kaldager, former head of the top-secret Norwegian intelligence group E14, told *Verdens Gang*. "They were open, benign and naive countries, easy to travel to, with good infrastructure and little police control. A lot probably happened that the public never heard about."

However, one factor involving state apparatus may explain why no record of the Oslo Woman can be found. If she was from the former East Germany, as many believe, her records might have been destroyed by the Stasi, the former Ministry for State Security. The ministry pulped hundreds of thousands of files during the period that saw the fall of the Berlin Wall and German reunification, including many birth records and police files.

This period of political chaos following the fall of the so-called Iron Curtain led to a considerable increase in crime in Germany and Eastern Europe, with weapons and organized crime flooding the market. Equally, as the German police force was purged of communist personnel, many precincts lost up to 40% of their officers. In 1991, neo-Nazi violence returned to the streets, with killings, beatings, and persecution of ethnic minorities and the gay community being pushed down the list of legal priorities. Following reunification, East Germany was far from the western paradise that many thought it would instantly become, and somebody fleeing the turmoil for better pastures in Norway is not unlikely.

Equally, given the amount of ammunition the woman had, the possibility exists that she had been planning a killing for reasons unknown. This may have been an action against an individual or even many. The poor condition of the gun and test into the pillow seems to discount a professional hit, and such a murder would have been a personal matter. While men primarily carry mass shootings, Sylvia Seegrist and the infamous Brenda *"I Don't Like Mondays"* Spencer show this is not a universal truth. Likely conflicted, "Jennifer" may have chosen to not carry out her plan.

The most likely explanation, however, is that the case was indeed a "simple" suicide. If the mystery woman had been in the country for a while, obtaining a gun might not be an issue. While using such a weapon in suicide is traditionally masculine, the man's aftershave and short hair may suggest the Oslo Woman might have been gender curious or displayed masculine traits. While "Lois" is a male name in French, it is female in English, and "Fairgate" is an English surname. Equally, the cologne may have been a reminder of lost love, perhaps connected with the Plaza Hotel as a place of significance in her past. She ensured that her identity would never be known, possibly believing that her loved ones might handle a disappearance better than suicide. Perhaps inspired by the famous Isdal Woman, she cut the tags from her clothes and began discarding her belongings about Oslo on her the time away from the room. She shot herself dead as security knocked on the door, never having time to get rid of the rest. Perhaps she believed it was the police and that she or the gun may be about to be discovered. Sadly, it may have been that the calls she failed to make to Belgium were the last cry for help.

Phantom image of the Oslo Woman by Harald Nygård for Oslo Police.

No matter the real reasons for the woman's death in Room 2805, somewhere out there, a mother has been waiting for her girl to come home for 25 years. Friends, brothers, and sisters wonder what happened to their beloved "Jennifer." While they retain hope they may see their loved one again and are spared the grief of the truth, they have no closure or moment of goodbye. We do not know their name nor their pain over a quarter of a century. Nor do we know the anguish of whatever it was that led to the events that fateful night in Oslo. While it may, in one way, seem cruel to snuff out this glimmer of hope, perhaps soon technology may allow the Oslo Woman's unknown family to know the truth and put a name on that anonymous grave at the Vestre Gravlund Cemetery.

15 THE ABDUCTION AND MURDER OF EMILIE MENG

Denmark, 2016

Located on the west coast of Denmark, Korsør is a small town of just 14,608 people, being a rising tourist destination in the country that is full of Scandinavian charm. However, darkness lingers over the place, with the unresolved murder of 17-year-old Emilie Meng in 2016 still haunting both local residents and the nation alike. Murders rarely go unsolved in Denmark, and the senseless killing of a regular Danish teenager shocked the country.

On July 10, 2016, Emilie Meng was last seen in Korsør, departing the train station and headed for home following a night out with friends in Slagelse, a town to the east. The friends celebrated their success in end-of-year exams that had concluded their first year at Slagelse Gymnasium, having achieved their high school diplomas. The atmosphere during the night was said by friends to be jubilant, with the three visiting a shisha cafe and McDonald's during their time out. The girls were described as kind, well-mannered and respectful. There was no suggestion that alcohol or drugs were involved during the night out or as a part of Emilie's life in a broader context. However, at McDonald's, the atmosphere changed, and Meng was said to have become upset when she received a Facebook message from a boy, ending their relationship. While the two were not a formal couple, there had been a developing interest, and Emilie was visibly upset.

Back in Korsør, it was around 4am when she said goodbye to her two friends who took a taxi; Emilie decided to walk the 2.5 miles to her home she shared with her parents and siblings. Meng continued to text her friends from her cellphone until her battery died, having told them she intended to take a road past some allotments and onto a small street between the station and highway.

"We drive past her in the taxi, and the last thing we see is that she is still walking on the path," friend Nicole Grundtoft told *Dagbladet*. "I think nothing is going to happen. It's Korsør; almost nothing happens here."

Emilie was expected to sing at church the following morning but never arrived, and a search by Emilie's mother failed to find the missing teenager. Upon raising the alarm, volunteers throughout the town assisted local police in scouring the area to find the missing girl. Despite the best efforts of locals, not a trace of Emilie was to be found. It was the most extensive volunteer search in Danish history, with hundreds turning out to find the young woman.

Out for their morning run, witnesses in Korsør reported that they observed a white van traveling at speed through the town in the early hours. The roads were narrow, and they were forced to leap aside, so they weren't mown down. Another witness says he saw what may have been the same van at a store just a few hundred yards from the train station. That afternoon, a fire broke out at a factory complex in the town that some speculated may have been connected with the missing girl. A 15-year-old boy was later arrested for arson. Police would also reveal their interest in a white Hyundai I30, 2011–2016 model. The car was seen driving around the station near the time of the disappearance.

The Police worked on three theories. One that she had taken off unexpectedly to stay somewhere else, likely as she was upset. Two that she had had an accident. Her root home took her across a canal, and there were theories she may have slipped and fallen in the water. Finally, she had become the victim of a crime. Sadly, as the weeks wore on, the optimism of those involved undoubtedly waned, and the third option looked increasingly likely. While there were tips, there were only around 45, with only three considered strong enough to identify a suspect. Those coming under suspicion included a 33-year-old truck driver and a 67-year-old who had his home searched on five separate occasions, with none of the information leading police anywhere. Police also analyzed mobile phone traffic around the area, identifying around 200 numbers they called "interesting."

Emilie Meng. Interpol photo.

However, it was later revealed that a data loss incident may have erased the killer's number alongside others that may have been active in the area at the time. It wouldn't be the only criticism of police handling the case, with authorities failing to secure surveillance footage that may have shown vehicles stated to be of interest and, equally, failing to question witnesses in the immediate aftermath of the disappearance. Police would defend their actions by saying they initially believed that Emilie had merely run away from home following the bad news she'd received on Facebook Messenger. The missing data was recovered in 2019 yet had possibly severely hampered the original investigation.

The truck driver from the Kolding area was under suspicion almost immediately after the disappearance. A former friend of the man reported him to police after a conversation that he found peculiar. The man had a previous conviction for a sexual offense against a minor and undoubtedly looked suitable for the crime. Such was the police's confidence; his home and garden were immediately searched for burial sites. The suspect was taken into custody and questioned by authorities in Slagelse, with his truck's GPS eventually proving he wasn't in Korsør on the night of Emilie Meng's disappearance.

"I'm sick of it. It's hurting my family, and I'm a little tired of it. And the reason I want to tell [the public] about it is that of course the police have to take reports seriously, but I think they made too big a deal out of it," the unnamed suspect told *BT*. "They should put two and two together and check my alibi before they come out with 16 men and search my home."

Despite his protestations, the truck driver would be arrested again for raping a nine-year-old girl in 2018.

The publicity surrounding the case prompted parents in Denmark to pick up their children to take them directly home or give them money for a taxi. There was even a local action group named The Night Ravens, mounting bicycles and stepping up citizen patrols around the train station where young men were noted as congregating to approach young girls. One group of vigilantes even believed they had found the girl, staking out a house and placing a citizen under surveillance as they publicly accused him of holding Emilie in his home. Some, such as former member Helle Flintholm, believed the action was self-defeating and immoral, contacting the police over the group's behavior.

"I suddenly find out that since August, an elderly couple has been monitored at an address in Korsør, because the neighbor thought that a woman's voice shouted for her mother and for help while knocking and kicking sounds have been heard," said Helle Flintholm, a former member of the vigilante group.

The police would state that while they understood the depth of feeling amongst the local community in Korsør, the vigilante group had gone too far, and the law needed to work in peace. The Missing Persons group subsequently agreed to stand down.

"We recommend that we be left in charge of the investigation of the missing Emilie Meng. That is what we are set in the world for, and we have both the tools and the training for it," said Police Inspector

Kim Kliver in a statement. "We, therefore, want to appeal to you to think really hard before you start running with loose rumors. It hurts both the investigation and Emilie's relatives. We are still working intensively to find out what may have happened on July 10. And we still have more directions we can move our investigation in."

The incident merely highlighted the intense emotions felt across the town and local area surrounding the case. However, not everyone was consumed by grief for the missing Emilie nor eager to aid in the search effort. The Offensimentum Facebook group has become notorious in Denmark for the content shared, often comparable to the likes of 4-Chan. Despite efforts of the admin team, numbering just 15 for 42,000 followers, the group became filled with memes and "jokes" at the expense of the girl, her disappearance being widely mocked. The postings perhaps show the nihilism of our age, one that crosses all borders around the globe.

Increasingly desperate for information, a personal and confidential number was launched to enable witnesses to report their suspicions anonymously, with a 200,000 kroner reward offered for details by the family. Emilie's details were passed to Interpol as police speculated she may have traveled abroad or even been abducted and taken across the border into Germany.

With three months gone in the case, developments seemed to be underway in October as it was revealed that a 67-year-old man had had his home searched in Korsør, police working on the theory that the girl had been kidnapped and was being held as a prisoner. The press would evoke the Natascha Kampusch affair that shocked the world ten years prior in 2006. The suspect, Finn Petersen, was the same suspect that had been highlighted by Missing Persons. He had his property searched on four separate occasions, with neighbors reporting they had heard screams and knocking from the house. The searches seemingly cleared Petersen of any involvement, with police suggesting that the publicity surrounding the case led to citizens misinterpreting innocuous events as suspicious. However, police would search the property again later that same month, drilling into the walls and the floor despite the comments. They would eventually eliminate Petersen from their inquiries once and for all, with the pensioner claiming he was the victim of harassment.

"I have been harassed so much, so they must have an ugly taste in their mouths," Petersen said to *Dagens DK*.

With the case file almost empty and little to go on, Emile seemed destined to be one of the innumerable missing girls and women across Denmark who are never found. However, on Christmas Eve, 2016, a passer-by walking his dog in a forested area of Regnemarks Bakke near Borup discovered the body of Emile; it had been submerged in a lake. Police believe the girl had been murdered shortly after disappearing on July 10 and subsequently dumped at the location around 40 miles from her home.

The discovery of the body brought in 250 new leads and tips from the public, but once again, there was little further in the case. The police still believed that the sightings of the white van immediately after the kidnapping were significant, as was the white Hyundai. Police confirmed that the lake was free from any forensic evidence that might have led them to Emile's killer. A torch-lit procession of remembrance was held for Emilie in Korsør before she was buried on January 19, 2017, at Skt. Povl's Church in the town, the church where she used to sing.

Since the discovery of Emilie Meng's body at Christmas 2016, the police have kept their cards close to their chest. They have revealed little of the investigation or investigators' findings, not even indicating how the 17-year-old was killed. The only hint of development was the press announcing that a witness saw somebody lifting a heavy object out of a white car near the lake where the body was discovered. After two years of near-silence on the matter, an anonymous source posted a letter to the offices of the Danish tabloid *BT*, which stated they had information on the case. The letter, which covered two sides of A4, revealed details about the affair that had never been made public. In January of 2019, police carried out DNA tests in Emilie's own neighborhood, perhaps suggesting that a new theory has taken hold in the case that leads closer to home than initially suspected.

In 2019, a 42-year-old man was arrested in connection with the murder. The man owned a white Hyundai, one of the vehicles that the police had been keen to trace. He was already in custody in connection to two other murders, both elderly men. The man confessed to killing 68-year-old coin collector Kiehn Andersen in Ruds Vedby in April and the murder of 80-year-old Poul Frank Jørgensen in Vemmelev in June. However, both murders have distinctly different features to Emilie Meng, both being elderly men stabbed in their own homes, which were subsequently burned down. However, one of the victims was taken from his house and thrown in a lake. The man was later dismissed from inquiries.

One new theory has also emerged that links "submarine killer" Peter Madsen to the case. Madsen, notorious for his murder of the Swedish journalist Kim Wall aboard his privately constructed submarine, has allegedly been looked at for Emilie Meng's murder on three separate occasions by Danish police. Investigators have highlighted several similarities in the killing of Wall and Meng, with Madsen known to have been driving a white van at the time of Emilie's abduction. Madsen is also said to have close links with Korsør, and the murder would have come less than a year before his murder of Wall. Madsen was described at his trial as a narcissistic psychopath who had been seen watching videos of decapitation and practicing asphyxiation sex by colleagues.

In 2021, information that stemmed from the broadcast of the Swedish documentary *Someone knows something about the murder of Emilie Meng* on Kanal 5 led to Danish police seizing a vehicle that belonged to Madsen.

In the documentary, two *BT* journalists, Bo Norström Weile and Jesper Vestergaard Larsen, seemingly found traces of blood in a van that Madsen leased in the years up to 2017, when police arrested him for the murder of Kim Wall. Like the one that features heavily in the Emilie Meng case, the van is white.

The documentary also features an interview with a fellow prisoner who alleges that Madsen admitted that he had killed other people, including one in Sweden and a young woman in Korsør.

After four years, it is difficult to judge how close the police are to a breakthrough in the case, with investigators going quiet ever since finding the body. The link to Madsen may seem based on supposition, yet recent investigations of his van and claims from a fellow prisoner may confirm what many had suspected, that being he had killed before. However, DNA tests locally, however, seem to suggest that a profile of the killer has been found somewhere and that police may no longer believe the murder to have been a random kidnapping.

With developments perhaps just around the corner, the case continues to provoke strong emotions in Denmark. Many question whether the police have the training or support to deal with such issues and whether Denmark's strict laws on surveillance are adequate in modern society. While these debates loom large, however, a killer possibly remains on the loose. Whether the attack was random or targeted, there has yet to be justice for Emilie Meng. Whether that's thanks to police failings or a frighteningly able killer remains open to debate. It is perhaps difficult to judge which would be worse.

"It was probably just a person who has driven by and thought she is beautiful and young and then taken her from us," Nicole Grundtoft said to *Dagbladet*. "If Emilie's killer is never found, it's going to break my heart. She deserves justice."

ABOUT THE AUTHOR

Michael East is a freelance writer based in the United Kingdom. With a background in history and politics, he has for many years written on a variety of topics, including both of those subjects alongside science-fiction, fantasy, unsolved mysteries, and of course, true crime.

When he's not writing about terrible murders, Michael wastes the rest of his time on video games, professional wrestling, and watching cute videos of cats to balance out the darkness.

Nordic Noir is his first book, and he is already working on a sequel.